_Pa_

Hi, my name is Mike. I wrote this book. I like to think that there is something in it for everyone, but some get more out of it than others. So, whether you purchased this book or received it as a gift, I hope you will read at least the first chapter and perhaps skim the others before deciding what to do with it. Read all or part of it, as you see fit, keep it, as long as it is helpful to you, and then pass it on to someone else. If you like, you may sign your name below so future recipients may see where it has been. Wishing you all the best, that God has to offer! May you experience the height and length and breadth of his amazing love for you! Thanks for your help!

Sincerely,

Mike

_____   _____

_____   _____

_____   _____

_____   _____

_____   _____

_____   _____

_____   _____

_____   _____

Drummer Boy's Lunchbox

Fish & Bread for Sinners & Saints;
The Twinkle-Twinkle in the Opus of God.

Mike Freed

2nd Revised,

Pass-Along Edition

R. Michael Freed
Wichita, Kansas

Copyright © 2014, 2020 by R. Michael Freed

All rights reserved. No part of this publication may be reproduced, distributed or transmitted in any form or by any means, without the prior written permission of the author, except in the case of brief quotations embodied in critical reviews and certain other noncommercial uses permitted by copyright law. In addition, the original purchasers of the book and those to whom it has been given may make copies of individual poems or passages to keep for themselves or share at no cost with others, provided that the following notice is included on the copy:
From Drummer Boy's Lunchbox
Copyright © 2014, 2020 by R. Michael Freed
mikefreed.xyz
.
(If your copy includes a bible passage please include the appropriate copyright information for that as well, Thank you!)

Scripture quotations marked (NIV) are taken from the Holy Bible, New International Version®, NIV®. Copyright © 1973, 1978, 1984, 2011 by Biblica, Inc.™ Used by permission of Zondervan. All rights reserved worldwide. www.zondervan.com The "NIV" and "New International Version" are trademarks registered in the United States Patent and Trademark Office by Biblica, Inc.™

Scripture quotations marked (WEB) are from the World English Bible and are a part of the Public Domain

Cover Illustration – Drummer Boy's Lunchbox - Copyright © 2019 by Mykayla Long, mykaylalong-art.com - License Secured

Book Layout ©2017 BookDesignTemplates.com

Library of Congress Control Number: 2020914197

Drummer Boy's Lunchbox / Mike Freed. —2nd Revised, Pass-Along Edition
ISBN: 9781723995453

*To My Father God, my Savior, Brother and Friend, Jesus, and the Good Spirit which dwells within us!
May the meditations of my heart and the words that I write, be acceptable and useful in Your sight!*

*To Linda, Elizabeth, and Rebekah!
My wife and daughters are such precious gifts!
Bringing me God's love!*

*To my former psychologist and still friend, Melissa!
You turned my life around! Many Thanks!*

*To My Readers!
May you be blessed! May you grow closer to God! May you be encouraged to love and live and forgive!
(and may you buy many copies of my book for your friends LOL)*

Contents

A Few Notes - You Can Read Now, Later or Not at All – You Decide! **13**

    Notes on the New Edition: 13

    The Illustrations and Photos 14

    Note on the New International Version (NIV): 15

Foreword **17**

    My Brother, Mike! 17

Points of Departure **19**

    Most Days Anyway 23

    Mike's Paradoxical Hope 24

    These are "Scriptures" 28

    So, What do You Think? 29

    Life 30

    Of Pearls & Poetry 31

    To ponder, journal and/or perhaps share: 32

Fish and Bread and Beautiful Music **35**

    Loaves and Fishes and Visionary Wishes 35

    What Are We Going to Do with All This Leftover Food, Why Does Someone Keep Playing Twinkle, Twinkle Little Star, and for Goodness Sake, Who is Pounding on Those Drums? 36

    To ponder, journal and/or perhaps share: 39

At the Sound of the Trumpet and Drum **41**

    Drummer Boy's Psalm 41

    Unconditional Surrender 42

    Prayer of the Faithful 43

    Now Is The Time! – Fish and Bread Revisited 43

    To ponder, journal and/or perhaps share: 46

Snapshots from the Family Album **49**

Strength & Beauty (Ode to Ralph and Alberta) 53
The Bull of the Woods is Dead (In Memory of Dad) 53
Little Boy Lost 53
Legacy of the Wolf 54
Wolf Child 54
The Ghosts of My Childhood 54
My Fathers Tears 55
In the Presence of the Accuser 55
But My Family Sucks! 56
To ponder, journal and/or perhaps share: 58

From "I do!" to "Been There and Done That!" 61
Linda's Love 62
A Child's Love 62
Precious Gifts 63
Tornado Child 63
Giraffe Cookies at 5:00 am 64
Victory 65
When I Grow Up 65
The Return of the Giraffe Cookies 66
Daddy God 66
Aftermath of a Snow Day at Papa's (with Morning and Evening assists from Grandma) 67
A Father's Love 68
Just One More Story, Daddy 69
Let Your Light Shine 70
To ponder, journal and/or perhaps share: 70

Reflections of Relentless Love 73
The Blind Men and the Elephant 73
Relentless, Everlasting Love 78
This Thing Called Love 79

- Dear Dyings 80
- Circle of Love 81
- Goliath's Boast 82
- Prophecy Revisited - The Seal is Broken........................... 82
- A Psalm of God's Relentless and Enduring Love 83
- To ponder, journal and/or perhaps share:......................... 84

Ruminations and Regurgitations of a Bipolar Mind 87
- Depression... 88
- Some Days 92
- Black Birds Wreaking Havoc (The Old Man Rails)........ 93
- Memories, Outlooks & Emotions...................................... 98
- A Note From Dad 98
- A Psalm of Desperation and God's Response................. 98
- Bipolar Beatitude.. 99
- Progress at Last 99
- Self-Talk 100
- Melancholy and Madness 101
- Glorious Day, Long Lonely Night.................................. 101
- A Joyful Heart 103
- The Philosopher's Unexpected Surprise 103
- Freedom at Last 104
- To ponder, journal and/or perhaps share:..................... 104

Pray, Praise, Give Thanks or Complain, but be Honest with God 107
- The Prayer of my Youth 107
- A Double Prayer for no Particular Reason................... 110
- Wild-Eyed Imaginings - I think God Told Me to Put This Here (but maybe not) 114
- To ponder, journal and/or perhaps share:..................... 126

Table Scraps 129

Taste and See 130
Rebekah's Prayer 130
In a Dry Land 130
From the Mouths of Babes: 131
Morning Walk 133
Pheasant Faith 135
Today's Reality, Tomorrows Hope 136
The Puzzle Sits Completed 136
In God's Time 136
To ponder, journal and/or perhaps share: 139

Baskets Full of Leftovers! 143
In Search of my Sunday School Jesus 144
This I Believe – Mike's Confession and Prayer 145
Another Confession and Prayer 147
God-Man Walking 149
A Song for Anna, Michael and Brent 149
Know-One 152
Echoes of the Lost 152
Children of the Wind 153
Any Less 153
Oh, Generous Father 154
Who will Speak Up 155
Lost Song 155
Will It Really Make a Difference? 156
Peter's Call 157
Humanity Discovered (Babel Revisited) 157
Faith and Fertilizer 158
Chess Board Analogies 159
Computer Comparisons 159
Eden Reopened 160

True Abundance 161
Show Us Yourself 162
I Am.. 163
Give Us Godly Impatience, Wisdom and Courage 163
Taste and See.. 165
Healing Light! - Mixed Metaphors: My High School English Teacher Would Not Approve 165
Unashamed.. 166
To ponder, journal and/or perhaps share:............................ 167

Overflow Since the First Edition..171
Oh Spirit Flame 172
Let's Make it a Good Day 172
Today 173
Each New Day.. 173
Poems.. 174
No One Reads Poetry Much Anymore 175
From Mundane to Miraculous... 175
Peggy with the Pigtails 176
Tears 176
Wendy the Weimaraner 177
The 101st Time's the Charm... 178
Some Friendly Advice to Husbands 178
From Defeat, Victory.. 180
This Thing Called Faith 181
This Thing Called Hope.. 182
Time Echoes... 183
Intentional Take-Aways from My Time in Therapy in More-or-Less Random Order.. 186
Puya raimondii 'Mike' 187
I Write Schmaltz... 188

    Boundaries 188
    Just for a Day or Two 190
    Visiting Ann 191
    Of Love and Lotteries 192
    Our Jesus 194
    Number our Days in Love! 195
    We Can Make a Difference 197
    I Choose 198
    Shalom My Friend! 199
    To ponder, journal and/or perhaps share: 200

The Doxology **203**

The Blessing **205**

Acknowledgments **207**
    The Honor Due 207
    Blessed is the One 208
    Morning Words 209

About the Author **211**

A Few Notes - You Can Read Now, Later or Not at All – You Decide!

Notes on the New Edition:

Over five years have passed since I published the first edition and I have continued to write. Most of my writing still springs from the pages of my journal, though I have penned a few things with more deliberate intent. I write mostly for myself. It is one of the ways I process things. It helps me discover things about myself, God, and people that I might otherwise overlook. Of course, I hope others will read and benefit from this book. I hope it will inspire and spark insights into who we are and into God's amazing love for us! And in my humanness, pride, and mania, I even dare to dream that what I have written will attain bestseller status and touch the lives of millions of people. (LOL) God, however, knows the plans he has for this book, and first and foremost it was probably to work changes in me and my life. Still, I would not have published it if I didn't think others could benefit from it. So, I put it out there and ask God to use it and bless it as he sees fit!

While I wanted to keep much of the original edition intact, I have made considerable changes and added many poems and other writings. The new edition is over 50 pages longer than the original. A few of the additions have found their way into chapters where they seemed to fit. The rest you will find in Chapter 11, "Overflow Since the First Edition." I have moved a few poems to new locations in the book. The introduction has been reworked and is now Chapter One. The "Forward" to the book is now the "Foreword" as it should be, but otherwise it has not changed. Though no less important, I have reworked and moved the acknowledgments to the back of the book.

I have corrected some errors and probably introduced new ones. Like the first edition, this one also could have benefited from professional editing or proofreading but those expenses were not in the budget, so I ask your indulgences and suggest you treat it as an exercise in acceptance, for we all bear imperfections and shortcomings in need of grace, acceptance and help.

One of the things made clear from the response to the first edition was that like all books, some people relate to this book more than others. Some bought or requested multiple copies to share with their friends, while others hardly gave it a second look and buried it away with other works in a box or on a bookcase. **Books are meant to be read, and I hope you will at least read the first chapter before deciding what to do with this one. Read as much or as little of the rest of it as you see fit, keep the book for as long as it is helpful and then pass it along to someone else.** I have included a form in the front of the book for this purpose. And while you're at it, consider sharing other works that may be collecting dust around your house.

Overall, I have stressed less and prayed more over this new edition. My prayers continue to be that God would use this book to draw myself and others closer to Him and to one another and I pray that through the work of His Holy Spirit, it will be good enough to accomplish that purpose!

The Illustrations and Photos

While flipping through a copy of the first edition of this book my granddaughter, Karlie (7 years old at the time) informed me that the book needed "illustrations!" So, proud, fun-loving grandpa that I am, I ask her if she would like to be the illustrator for the revised edition. She agreed with the stipulation that the drawings must include at least one unicorn. I accepted and told her that I would pay her for the project. She was all-in! However, when she found out her drawings would be in black and white, she balked! Leaving me to work on "illustrations" of my own.

Not given to artistic talents, I relied heavily on the use of several photo editors and a ready supply of creative commons licensed photos on pixabay.com. To the degree that finance would allow, I have made donations to these artists and photographers who have so generously made their works available for use and I gratefully acknowledge their contribution to this book.

When all was said and done, Karlie and I reached a compromise, and this became a joint endeavor. By using the same photo editors, I turned some of her colorful drawings into black and white renderings and she allowed me to include them in the book along with the ones I had created. She also discovered one of the photo apps, PicSay Pro allowed her to create pictures and we have used some of those images as well. Most recently she has been painting pictures outlined by Paint the Town – Wichita, KS. Black and white editions of three of her colorful paintings have been included.

Sometime later, I met artist and illustrator, Mykayla Long at my church and she agreed to design the cover illustration for the book. You may explore more of her creations at mykaylalong-art.com.

Note on the New International Version (NIV):

I chose to use the NIV, because it was the version of the Bible I was reading when I began this project, many years ago, and because it has liberal usage rights. The NIV however has sometimes changed its wording from one edition to the next. In keeping with the current copyright restrictions for the NIV, all the Bible passages in this revised edition of Drummer Boy's Lunchbox have been updated to the latest,

2011 edition of the NIV, even though in a few cases I would have preferred to stay with an earlier version. Occasionally I have used the public domain World English Bible (WEB) or my own slightly modified version of it, and those have been indicated. At any rate, if the NIV scriptures quoted here look different from your NIV, it is probably because I have quoted the verse from the later edition.

Happy Reading!

Foreword

<u>My Brother, Mike!</u>

He bared his soul for all to see.
He bared his soul my brother, he.
He bared his soul for me to see,
That my brother, he is just like me.

The treasure he had, he shared with me,
His treasure gladly I share with thee.
His treasure when shared, multiplies abundantly,
Now and through eternity.

The treasure in its simplicity, "God is Love!"
God loves you and God loves me!

Mike said, for now, he would just rest in God's arms,
I think God might say, "And who is he, that Mike tells me,
Just what will be? I tell you it's up to me!"

So, to that, I say, "We'll see!"

Steve

A poem is a prayer that touches the heart,
A parenthesis that explains,
A parable of another world,
A mystery that's plain.

Like fine wine and vinegar,
Like the brewer's best and yeasty swill,
Like Kimchi and spoiled kraut,
Such are the fermentations of a bipolar heart and mind,
All things with purpose in their proper time,
Whether or not they seem to rhyme.
And much depends on taste.
Bon Appetit!

I will open my mouth with a parable; I will utter hidden things, things from of old— things we have heard and known, things our ancestors have told us. We will not hide them from their descendants; we will tell the next generation the praiseworthy deeds of the Lord, his power, and the wonders he has done.
(Psalm 78:2-4 NIV)

Chapter One

Points of Departure

Dear friends, let us love one another, for love comes from God. Everyone who loves has been born of God and knows God. Whoever does not love does not know God, because God is love. This is how God showed his love among us: He sent his one and only Son into the world that we might live through him. This is love: not that we loved God, but that he loved us and sent his Son as an atoning sacrifice for our sins. Dear friends, since God so loved us, we also ought to love one another. No one has ever seen God; but if we love one another, God lives in us and his love is made complete in us.
(1 John 4:7-12 NIV)

I am an aging fat man. My life has been less than remarkable and successful by many standards, but I am beginning to know and appreciate the amazing, relentless, passionate love God has for me and all people! To paraphrase Brennan Manning, He loves me, he loves you, he loves everyone just as they are and not as they should be, because in this life, none of us are or ever will be as we should be! God's love is unconditional, undeserved, and unfathomable! Indeed, I suspect with the apostle John that **"God is love" and our purpose is to live in that love and love one another!**

If you have skimmed this book at all, you probably already know that I consider myself a beloved child of God and a follower of Jesus Christ by the power of the Holy Spirit working within me. Though I often sin and fall short, this is the realm in which I tend to live and a bias from which I approach things. There are many things in the Bible and the teachings and history of the Christian church that I do not understand; things I wrestle with or even rebel against; things attributed to God that often seem incompatible with my limited concept of a loving God. At times, I weep or am appalled by the sins and atrocities that have been committed throughout the ages in the name of Jesus! He would not approve! Yet, much good has also been done in that name, and I have found scripture and the church's teachings, especially the words of Jesus, helpful and life changing.

My journey of faith has often been difficult and painful, and I have not yet "arrived." I don't have "it" all figured out. I continue at times to struggle and to strive. The words of scripture, of Jesus, though often comforting also confront and convict me, as I realize how I have "missed the mark" and how much I need God, how much I need Jesus!

There were (and perhaps occasionally still are) times in my life when I was angry with God, hostile toward God, or even doubted he existed. God is patient, however, and He continues to work in my life; molding and shaping me into the person he would have me to be. I do my best to love others. I try often unsuccessfully, to discern God's leading and to follow where he leads. I like to think that he has led me to produce this revised edition of the Drummer Boy's Lunch Box; that he has guided my words and that he will continue to use them to accomplish His good and saving purpose.

One of the things I have discovered about myself is that I am and probably always have been a "hopeful Christian universalist." I am hopeful that somehow through the saving work of his Son Jesus Christ and the working of His good and Holy Spirit, God will save all people and that one day beyond this time and space, all people will live in harmony, unity and community with God and all things (whether this is indeed possible or even desirable, I leave in His hands). While in my opinion there are places in scripture (John 12:32, Philippians 2:9-

11, Psalm 145:9-13, Isaiah 25:6-9, Isaiah 45:22-25, Romans 5:18, 1 Timothy 2:3-6 for example) that seem to suggest all will be saved, and while it is the sincere hope to which I feel God's Spirit has led me, I would be remiss if I did not also say that scripture, traditional church doctrine (if there is anything left of that), and Jesus' own words are also full of warnings to the contrary. Warnings which state that what we believe, the decisions we make, the words we speak, the things we think and do and don't do are of importance, perhaps utmost importance both for the here and now and for eternity! (So, walk carefully! Judge for yourself!) How can both things be true? I do not know! I suspect it is either a paradox, one of those mystical unexplainable, seemingly impossible realities that just is, or a mistaken idea born out of my desire not to condemn anyone including myself.

So, where does this leave us? My answer is, to not take God's grace for granted and to leave the decisions of who is and isn't "saved" in God's wise, merciful, and just hands! In my opinion, none of us get to heaven on our own merits. It is only by God's grace and mercy in the work of His Son, Jesus, and by the power of His Holy Spirit that any of us can believe and trust in God or be saved. It is a gift! It is pure undeserved love and mercy! A theology professor I once had said something to the effect that "the great mystery is not will all be saved but how any of us are saved!" If God can love an old, washed-up, fat man like me, if he can claim the often messed up characters in the Bible as his own, then just perhaps he can and will somehow save everyone. That is my great hope and prayer, but let's not take it for granted!

Therefore, as God's Spirit leads and enables you, turn to God (repent) and trust God; believe in Jesus and follow his teachings; and extend love, kindness, mercy, justice, and forgiveness to those around you! You don't have to have everything figured out or believe all the right things to begin this process. Live in and share God's undeserved love and forgiveness! This is important both for the here and now and for eternity! **Live in God's undeserved love, walk with Him and let him live in you and change you and help you wrestle with and resolve all the fears and hurts, the angers, sorrows, and questions of your heart and mind. Be honest with God, he already knows you better than you know yourself. Let him love you with both the tender and tough love of a kind and wise father and of a faithful older brother, savior, and friend! Let His good and transforming Spirit change you and open your heart to Himself and those around you! Bask in God's love and forgiveness and then love and forgive those around you!**

I hope many types of people will read this book and find it helpful. I hope it will encourage them to further explore and embrace Jesus as savior, teacher, and friend! I hope it will draw them closer to God, to His Son and to each other, whether they can fully accept the teachings of the Christian faith or not. A couple of groups of people deserve special mention here.

First Atheists, who don't even believe that God exists (and I have felt that way at times). Let me ask you a couple of questions? Consider this book, or your computer, or your cellphone, or a host of other objects, would you ever believe that these things appeared on their own without a creator? How then can you believe that things infinitely more complex such as the human body, the solar system, or the universe, arose on their own without an intelligent creator? Think about it!

Second. for those of us, who are "Christians," "religious types," "good church people," and/or "believers," (and I include myself in all these categories) a special caution is in order. We need to remind ourselves that Jesus reserved his sternest warnings for the "religious types," the "good church people" and the "believers," of His day. These people were so concerned about believing and doing things right, that they often failed to do the right thing and to extend God's love, kindness, mercy, justice, and

forgiveness to others. In the process, they may have shut the door to the kingdom of heaven to themselves and those around them. Dear brothers and sisters, let us not be guilty of the same sin and let us also remind ourselves that the quality that identifies us to the world as Christ's followers is not the purity of our doctrine (as important as that may be), it is not the unity of our teachings, but the love we have for one another!

> *"A new command I give you: Love one another. As I have loved you, so you must love one another. By this everyone will know that you are my disciples, if you love one another." (John 13:34-35 NIV)*
>
> *"...I urge you to live a life worthy of the calling you have received. Be completely humble and gentle; be patient, bearing with one another in love. Make every effort to keep the unity of the Spirit through the bond of peace. There is one body and one Spirit, just as you were called to one hope when you were called; one Lord, one faith, one baptism; one God and Father of all, who is over all and through all and in all." (Ephesians 4:1-6 NIV)*
>
> *This is love: not that we loved God, but that he loved us and sent his Son as an atoning sacrifice for our sins. Dear friends, since God so loved us, we also ought to love one another... We love because he first loved us. Whoever claims to love God yet hates a brother or sister is a liar. For whoever does not love their brother and sister, whom they have seen, cannot love God, whom they have not seen. And he has given us this command: Anyone who loves God must also love their brother and sister. (1 John 4:10-11, 19-21)*

Most Days Anyway

I don't understand it all, but I believe and trust (most days anyway) in a God bigger and wiser and more loving and caring and forgiving than myself!

I believe in and trust, and respect and try to follow (most days anyway) a man, a God-Man who loves us and laid down his life for us and said, "Father forgive them!" and rose again and promises new, abundant and eternal life.

I believe and trust (most days anyway) in a good and transforming Spirit that dwells within us and engulfs us and encourages us and empowers us to be the beloved and loving children of God that we were meant to be!

Mike's Paradoxical Hope

Abba Father, Abba Lord,
My strong deliverer, my Rock, and my Sword!
We cross the raging streams of life, to go as Joshua went,
Destroying all the evil ones, but were their lives really spent?
For though I don't understand it, I believe we're kept by God,
And that in the end we'll walk the walk and tread where Enoch trod!
But were there not two Enochs, one evil and one good?
So, choose your road with caution, but this also is assured...
He loves us with an infinite love and God is not too small -
To save every single one of us - did He not die for all!
But again, I must remind you to choose your path with care,
For real and present is the danger,
Satan lurks everywhere!
And He would steal you from the Father!
He would catch you in his snare!
He would devour and destroy you and catch you unaware.
For though our salvation is certain, and bears a cross-shaped seal,
Yet, ever-present is the danger, ever-present, and for real!

> **"Follow God's example, therefore, as dearly loved children and walk in the way of love, just as Christ loved us and gave himself up for us as a fragrant offering and sacrifice to God ... For you were once darkness, but now you are light in the Lord. Live as children of light (for the fruit of the light consists in all goodness, righteousness and truth) and find out what pleases the Lord. Have nothing to do with the fruitless deeds of darkness, but rather expose them... Be very careful, then, how you live—not as unwise but as wise, making the most of every opportunity, because the days are evil. Therefore,**

do not be foolish, but understand what the Lord's will is."
(Ephesians 5:1-2, 8-11, 15-17 NIV)

"Be alert and of sober mind. Your enemy the devil prowls around like a roaring lion looking for someone to devour. Resist him, standing firm in the faith, because you know that the family of believers throughout the world is undergoing the same kind of sufferings. (1 Peter 5:8-9 NIV)

You may also find it helpful to know from the start that I have firsthand experience with mental illness. I live my life with a condition called bipolar affective disorder, sometimes referred to as manic depression. Characterized by swings between periods of extreme depression, exuberant highs, high energy, angry mixed states, more-or-less "normal states" and everything in between; it has, to say the least, often caused problems in my life. I have also experienced debilitating panic and anxiety attacks. I have been fortunate that God's grace, often in the form of good medications, good doctors and counselors, learned coping skills and the support of family and friends, has mitigated the effects of these tyrants. None the less, they have at times extracted a heavy toll. Still, I consider myself one of the lucky ones, as bipolar disorder is one of the more treatable mental illnesses and lately, most days are good days.

Often people afflicted with bipolar disorder, especially when they are manic, feel a special closeness to God. They may even think they are God, the Christ, or a prophet of God. I have indeed flirted with these thoughts and feelings myself. Coming down from manic episodes can wreak havoc on one's faith. Trying to discern what is real and what is fantasy; what is revelation and what is rubbish; what to hang on to and what to let go of is not an easy task. On the other end of the spectrum, I have felt utterly worthless, felt like God had deserted me, was angry with me, or didn't even exist. And yes, I have been angry with God! More than once I was tempted to discard my faith altogether, but God kept drawing, or perhaps dragging, me back.

All of us (or at least Christians) live with another kind of bipolar disorder; the disorder that we are both sinners and saints. We struggle with the old sinful self, while at the same time we are new creations completely holy in Christ. These two natures often war within us causing conflict, confusion, inconsistency, and strife.

You will find both these bipolar conditions expressed and intermingled in my writings. These writings reflect my life's journey, though they are not arranged chronologically. They are a collage and kaleidoscope of my past and present and my hopes for the future. They certainly don't paint a systematic theology or doctrine. They express my thoughts, beliefs, and emotions at the time they were written, which may have changed over time. So, read carefully and with God's guidance, decide for yourself what is true or right or helpful.

I gave up theology (the study of God) a while ago. Trying to figure God out can drive you crazy. I believe it played at least a part in my first hospitalization for mania. Our minds simply can't fully comprehend God. We try to build bigger and better boxes, confessions, and creeds, to contain or explain Him. While such things may be helpful to us in grasping the infinite, God refuses to be fully contained, constrained, or explained by them. His ways simply are not our ways; they are much better! To be clear, I have not given up the study of God's word. Each day it inspires me or reveals to me something new or remembered about God and His great love for us. However, most days, rather than trying to figure God out, I am content just to grow and rest in His love and forgiveness and to do what I can to share them with others.

I'll leave you with a few more thoughts, poems and scriptures before I move on. I hope they give you at least a little more insight into how best to approach the rest of this book.

First, **you don't have to read the book in the order it is written or from cover to cover; feel free to jump around and explore.** While I hope you enjoy and grow from my poems and other writings,

I especially commend to you the Bible passages contained in this book. If they cause you to want to read more of the Bible, I suggest you begin with one of the "gospels," Matthew, Mark, Luke or John (my favorite is John), for these contain the works and words of Jesus while he was on earth among us. As I said above, **you don't have to have Jesus all figured out to benefit from his teachings.** Let his words and the words of those who knew Him best sink deep into your soul and let His Spirit transform you and draw you to Himself and to the Father. If you have questions take them to God; if something convicts you, confess it to God. **One of the key messages of the Bible is to repent. Repent means to turn around.** By nature, we often turn away from God, but by the power of His Holy Spirit working within us we are also able to turn towards God. **Turning back to God has made so much difference in my life and the lives of many others. When you do something wrong, turn to God for forgiveness and help; if you have questions, concerns, or cares, take them to God; if you find yourself consumed by anger, hatred, fear, or other emotions; go to God for help. Having trouble believing in God, lay your case before Him! Be honest with God! God loves you more than you can even begin to imagine! Though it may not always seem like it, He has your best interest and the best interest of all people at heart!**

Life is a journey filled with questions. A journey filled with problems and pitfalls. A journey filled with people, people who can be hard to love and live with. My experience is that this journey, though sometimes hard is much easier, much more enjoyable and more rewarding with God as our traveling companion, especially if we let Him lead us where He would have us to go.

If something I have written offends you, examine yourself closely or discuss it with friends, for that which upsets us most, often strikes at the heart of who we are, or it may simply be "new wine" that you are trying to put into old wineskins. As Jesus reminded us (Mathew

9:17) new wine will burst old wineskins. So, if you are able, allow God to create new "wineskins," new paradigms, new mindsets and let things ferment a bit, coming back occasionally to test them and to see if they have aged into something palatable and delicious. Often after new wine ages we find that it can be mixed with old wine for an even more pleasing drink.

Mary, Jesus' mother, set us a good example of how to deal with things we cannot fully understand or accept. If you can, take this attitude:

> *But Mary treasured up all these things and pondered them in her heart. (Luke 2:19 NIV)*

If you simply cannot get by something, I suggest you mark through it with a black marker or just tear it out, shred it, wad the remains in a ball, and propel it towards the nearest trash can; then move on. It is much healthier than fretting or fuming over it.

These are "Scriptures"

These are "scriptures," for scriptures are writings and that is what these are.

These are "holy scriptures," for holy means "set apart" and scriptures are "writings" and that is what these are. "Writings" "set apart" to give God glory and to proclaim His immeasurable love and forgiveness made manifest in His Son, Jesus Christ.

These are "inspired holy scriptures," for inspired means "God-breathed" and holy means "set apart" and "scriptures" are writings, and that is what these are. "Writings" "set apart" to give God glory and to proclaim His immeasurable love and forgiveness made manifest in His Son, Jesus Christ. "Scriptures" which in the process of their writing, God used to "breathe" new life into the writer, whose hope and prayer is that God will use these "scriptures "to breathe new life into you as well (provided of course that, you inhale deeply and hold your nose on occasion).

Please understand that I do not mean to imply that my writings are inspired in the same way that many believe the Bible is inspired. However, it is my earnest prayer that God will use them to inspire you and renew your faith, hope, and love.

So, What do You Think?

What do you think of my writings? Do they have anything to say?
I hope they make you think a bit and help you on your way.
But if we don't see eye to eye, in style, thought or philosophy,
Then perhaps in love, we can keep seeking, until at last we see,
The I in you and you in me!

To help you "think a bit" and to hopefully "help you on your way" I have included questions at the end of most chapters. I hope you will take time to ponder and answer them, use them as journaling prompts (I highly recommend journaling), and/or share your responses with others, either in informal discussions or perhaps group settings. Such discussions can be helpful in seeing the differences, similarities, and uniqueness that God has built into each of us. This is at least a part of seeing and appreciating the "I in you and you in me!" Though placed at the end of each chapter, you may find it helpful to read through the questions before reading the chapter.

Finally, they say that "attitude is everything." Though perhaps not everything, the attitude with which we approach something can make a big difference, as the following story and poem illustrate. The poem is original the story is not. The story has been told and retold in various forms. I wish I knew who originated it, so that I could give them credit.

Anyway, as the story goes some scientists were conducting an experiment in human behavior. The scientists took two boys and placed them in separate rooms. In the room with the first boy they placed every kind of toy, and electronic gadget you can imagine. The room with the second boy was filled waist-deep with horse manure.

The scientists left and came back later. When they entered the first room, they found all the toys had been broken or cast aside and the first boy crying and complaining that he was bored and that there was nothing to do. When they entered the room with the second boy, to their amazement, they found the lad joyfully singing and slinging manure everywhere. When they inquired into the boy's unusual behavior, he replied simply,

"With all this poop there has to be a pony in here somewhere!"

Life

Live and love expectantly-
For the poop you step in may lead you to a pony.
Amidst the stones that bruise your head or heel,
You may find a precious gem,
In the slime of oysters, a priceless pearl.

> **"The kingdom of heaven is like treasure hidden in a field. When a man found it, he hid it again, and then in his joy went and sold all he had and bought that field. Again, the kingdom of heaven is like a merchant looking for fine pearls. When he found one of great value, he went away and sold everything he had and bought it."**
> **(Matthew 13:44-46 NIV)**

Read the rest of this book expectantly! I'm sure you will find a pony or some other treasure in there somewhere. More importantly, **remember, you are God's precious treasure! He relentlessly seeks you and has given up everything, even His very life for you!**

Of Pearls & Poetry

Oh, precious pearl, oh pearl of great price,
My hidden treasure, my love, and my life!
I slip into poetry. I slip into song,
For great is my God, my strength to go on!

Jesus is my precious pearl, but more important I am His,
He loves me with an everlasting love, that's just the way it is!
He bought me back from Satan, with His holy precious blood,
And ascended into heaven to prepare a place above!

If I but trust in Him and all He's done and does for me,
I know that I will get through life, I can hardly wait to see...
To see Him face to face, without any fear,
To see Him smile and beckon me, to come closer and draw near!

My poems, they are simple, they may not be the best.
Others may criticize, make fun, or even jest.
But they come from deep within me, just where I do not know.
It seems that sometimes, all at once, they just seem to flow!

Some of my poems don't rhyme, and some are but endless clatter,
But I write them anyway, it really doesn't matter -
For my God sees and knows and cares,
And so, I send my poems and prayers, into the air, for my God cares!
He dares to care - for one so broken as I am.

> **Have mercy on me, O God, according to your unfailing love; according to your great compassion blot out my transgressions. Wash away all my iniquity and cleanse me from my sin ... a broken and contrite heart you, God, will not despise. (Psalm 51:1-2, 17b NIV)**

Father,
Use this book to bring light and life, healing, and comfort to Your people! Forgive us and give us joy and hope!

Draw us unto yourself and teach us to love one another!
In Jesus Name! Amen!

To ponder, journal and/or perhaps share:

1. If you were to write a book, what would be some of the "points of departure" that would be helpful to readers in understanding you and your point of view?

2. What is something you treasure? Why is it important?

3. What is one "bias" from which you approach things?

4. How would you describe yourself; what "type" of person are you?

5. Do you tend to be optimistic/positive or pessimistic/negative? Why do you suppose that is?

6. Do you look at yourself more as a "sinner" or a "saint"? Why is that?

7. What are some of the things about "traditional Christianity" that draw you closer to God or push you away from Him? Are there other things that keep you from believing in or trusting God? What are they?

8. What "poop" have you stepped in that eventually led you to a "pony"?

9. How has mental illness impacted your life or the lives of those around you?

10. What is one "box" you have tried to put God in?

11. What are some of the main pieces in the "collage" of your life? If your life was a kaleidoscope what would be some of the predominant colors and shapes? Why is that?

12. What inspires you?

13. When you hear the name Jesus what are your first thoughts? What do you believe right now about Him?

14. What are some of your thoughts and beliefs about, heaven, hell, salvation, eternal life, etc?

15. Do you tend to turn toward God or away from Him? Why do you suppose that is?

16. What is your initial impression of the author? What things (if any) make you want to read more? What things (if any) make you want to close the book for good?

Created with a Pixabay image from Pexels

Created with a Pixabay Image from fancycrave1

Created with a Pixabay Image from Alexas_Fotos

Chapter Two

Fish and Bread and Beautiful Music

... Jesus looked up and saw a great crowd coming toward him... "Andrew, Simon Peter's brother, spoke up, "Here is a boy with five small barley loaves and two small fish, but how far will they go among so many?" (John 6:5, 9 NIV)

Loaves and Fishes and Visionary Wishes

Oh Lord, let me dream Your dreams, and let me see with Your eyes,
For where there is no vision, it seems the people die.
Oh Lord, make me a force life-giving,
Your vision, light, and life to share.
Oh, holy God, please keep us, here and everywhere.
We know not what lies before us,
Whether humble things or great.
Please keep us, good Father. Save us before it's too late!
Too late to do the things we dreamed of,
Too late to say we're sorry!
Too late to offer hope or comfort, let's not wait until tomorrow.
To say that "I love you!" or to give someone a hug!
Today is our salvation! It began with Your Son!
And now we're called to pass it on,
In thought and word and deed.
To reach out and touch those many lives, in varied states of need,

But Lord, I'm just one person! What can one person do?
I'll offer up my fish and bread and leave the rest to You!

What Are We Going to Do with All This Leftover Food, Why Does Someone Keep Playing Twinkle, Twinkle Little Star, and for Goodness Sake, Who is Pounding on Those Drums?

In the story of the feeding of the 5000, a boy shares his lunch of two small fish and a few small loaves of bread. Jesus blesses it and has His disciples distribute it to the waiting multitude. When everyone has eaten their fill, they gather up 12 large baskets of leftover food. "Conservative" and "liberal" theologians would differ as to what was going on here. Some say that Jesus miraculously multiplied the gift of the young boy; others say that the example set by Jesus and the young lad moved the hearts of the people to share what they had brought; and a few ask insightfully, which is the greater miracle?

My question, though less profound, is: What do you think they did with all that leftover food? Did they use it to feed the poor? Did they eat off of it for the rest of the week or month? I have no idea, but I can't help but wonder if it wasn't given back to the boy who started the whole thing.

Then the question is, what did he do with all that leftover food? Did he get some help to carry it home to feed his family? Did he give it to the poor? Or did he sell it and start a Fish and Bread Enterprise? We'll never know.

I've heard it said that, "You can't out-give God." Sometimes, I struggle with that statement. I often cling tightly to the things that God has given me, especially money, but I am learning that as I give back to God and share with others, not only are they blessed, but I am blessed in return. It's no magical formula and sometimes the blessing is other than what we give. We don't always see an immediate return, nor should we give expecting one.

Two Bible passages come to mind:

Cast your bread on the waters; for you shall find it after many days. Give a portion to seven, yes, even to eight; for you don't know what evil will be on the earth. (Ecclesiastes 11:1-2 WEB)

*"Give, and it will be given to you. A good measure, pressed down, shaken together and running over, will be poured into your lap. For with the measure you use, it will be measured to you."
(Luke 6:38 NIV)*

What we give always returns to us in God's proper timing, whether it's money, or simple kindness. What can you give today, a word of encouragement; an act of forgiveness, mercy, or reconciliation; or a gift of money? Can you take a friend to lunch, or buy lunch for a homeless person, and maybe sit with him and give him the gift of your time and attention? Can you play with your children or spend time with your spouse? Can you visit someone in a nursing home or prison? Can you write a letter, send a card, connect with someone on Facebook, or make that long-overdue phone call?

Often, we are tempted to think that our humble efforts don't matter or that they pale in comparison to the works of others. I am reminded of the often-told story of a little boy who at his mother's insistence was reluctantly taking piano lessons. Thinking it might inspire and motivate the lad, she took him to see the performance of a famous concert pianist.

Before the performance began, while the mother was talking to some friends, the little boy wandered away. Going through a door marked "Stage Entrance," he found himself in front of a huge and beautiful grand piano and sat down to play.

As he plunked out his rendition of "Twinkle, Twinkle Little Star," suddenly the curtain went up and the spotlights came on. The boy's mother gasped in horror. At the same moment, the great pianist walked on stage. Approaching the boy from behind, he whispered, "Don't stop, keep playing, you're doing great, keep going!" Then reaching around on either side of the little tyke, he began playing. Adding counter melodies and harmonies, the result was nothing less than sensational. They concluded the piece to a standing ovation!

I am reminded also of another little boy, the little drummer boy in the Christmas carol by the same name. Having no gift to bring for the new-born baby king, Jesus, he simply played his drum for Him. And then to his amazement, the baby smiled at him in approval.

This book, as our entire lives should be, is a "Fish and Bread Project!" It is me playing my drums for Jesus! It is part of my Twinkle-Twinkle around which Christ the master plays and in which all people and the company of heaven join in! Every kind word and action are fish and bread in the master's hands; they are melodies around which God writes and performs His Opus! When we take the gifts and talents God has given us, no matter how seemingly small or insignificant they may be and offer them back to Him, He blesses them, multiplies them, and uses them as He sees fit.

My hope is that He will use this book and my life to feed many in both body and spirit. First, I hope all who read it will be fed spiritually. Secondly, I hope to donate most of the royalties to mission partners who provide food and other resources to the poor.

Whether God chooses to use this book and my life to touch the lives of a few or thousands or even more is up to Him. Though we are not always privileged to see it, all of us and all things have a part to play in God's plan. I believe that He takes even the trouble, pain, sorrow, and evil in our world and works it out for good. If He can work evil out for good, he can certainly use our efforts as well!

So, keep playing! Keep going! You're doing great! Offer up your fish and bread! Open your lunch box and share your food! Beat your drum, play on your piano, or sing your song! Whether you play Mozart or Chopsticks; whether your instrument is drums, piano, or voice; whether you can conduct a symphony or simply tap your foot in time and hum along; offer it up to God! He can use it! He can do more with it than you could ever imagine! So, keep playing! Keep going! You're doing great! Share your gifts! Play your song! Give as it has been given to you, a little or a lot, and ask for God's blessing upon it! Your life is not insignificant! Your gifts and your actions will not return to you void but will accomplish God's purpose! They will return and bring an increase in your life and the lives of others! So, share your music; share your lunch; share your life!

> *May God be gracious to us and bless us and make his face shine on us - so that your ways may be known on earth, your salvation among all nations. May the peoples praise you, God; may all the peoples praise you. May the nations be glad and sing for joy...*
> *(Psalm 67:1-4 NIV)*

To ponder, journal and/or perhaps share:

1. Whom do you most relate to, the boy who shared his lunch, the boy playing twinkle-twinkle or the little drummer boy? Why?

2. What is something you have always dreamed of doing, but never have?

3. Is there someone you wished to apologize to but never did? Is it too late to do that now?

4. To whom do you need to say, "I love you."?

5. What is one situation, where you say, "But Lord, I'm just one person, what can one person do?" What is one small thing that you can do? Remember to ask God to bless it!

6. Recall a time you received back more than you gave.

7. In what endeavors is God reaching around you to play along with you and encourage you to keep going?

8. What have been some of the predominant melodies in your life to this point? Do you wish to keep playing them or would you prefer with God's help to learn a new piece?

9. What "Fish and Bread Project" is God calling you to start today?

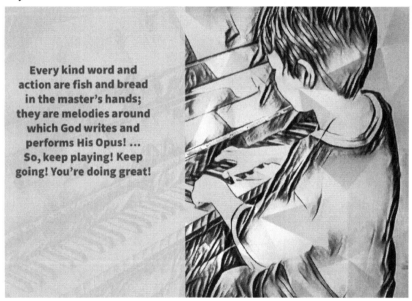

Created with a Pixabay Image from nightowl

Image by Karlie

Image created with PicSay Pro by Karlie

Chapter Three

At the Sound of the Trumpet and Drum

"For I know the plans I have for you," declares the Lord, "plans to prosper you and not to harm you, plans to give you hope and a future. Then you will call on me and come and pray to me, and I will listen to you. You will seek me and find me when you seek me with all your heart. I will be found by you," declares the Lord, "and will bring you back from captivity..." (Jeremiah 29:11-14 NIV)

Drummer Boy's Psalm

Turn me around and set me on a firm path, a path that leads to You; a path that leads to abundant life, now and in eternity.

You are a great God and greatly to be praised! Therefore, I will shout and sing of Your goodness and greatness! I will shout with joy! I will move forward in the midst of my enemies, as a troop advancing against a foe, as a drummer boy leading the charge!

You send Your enemies to flight. They flee before You. Who can stand? They cry out for mercy, they surrender unconditionally, and You forgive them all their wrongs! Everyone who turns to You, You pardon and call son or daughter. Those who do not turn, fall on their own sword. Even then, You rescue the dying and raise the repentant.

Only the fool turns away. Only the one marked for destruction, will not turn. He is a liar and a thief! He stirs the people against God! How lonely will be his desolation, all because he would not turn to his maker. How pitied he is among men, how lost among the holy ones. He was given great authority and power, lifted up on high, yet he used that to do evil, to spread rebellion and discord against our God. He would not repent of his evil ways and so they were his destruction!

But you, oh man, when you hear God's call, when you hear the sound of the drums and trumpets in the distance; turn around and return to the Lord your God! Confess your rebellion and hard-heartedness and plead for mercy! For the God, who advances before you, is merciful and will pardon you and restore your fortunes.

Do not perish with the evil one! Yield to the Spirit within you! Let Him turn you around and restore you to the Father! He will return you to the Father's camp! He will heal your wounds and forgive all your transgression! He will restore your fortunes! Today, when you hear His voice, turn around and run to your Father, who is running to meet you!

Unconditional Surrender

What shall I do with You, Jesus?
Your words are often hard, but Your heart is soft.
You play tenderly with children and invite them to come.
Then You rip the Pharisees up one side and down the other,
And condemn their duplicitous nature.
I am condemned also by Your words.
I cannot measure up to Your high standards.
Where shall I find peace?
I will "sue for peace" for I cannot overcome You.
I surrender unconditionally.
Your words are most gracious.
Go in peace! Forgive one another! Love one another!

> **"Or suppose a king is about to go to war against another king. Will he not first sit down and consider whether he is able with ten thousand men to oppose the one coming against him with twenty thousand? If he is not able, he will send a delegation while the other is still a long way off and will ask for terms of peace."**
> **(Luke 14:31-32 NIV)**

Prayer of the Faithful

Oh Father, whom I serve, my good most divine,
I break into poetry; I break into rhyme.
You are the one and only, at least You are to me,
Oh Father, grant me faith to act, and faith to believe.
For in action, I live out Your love,
And in believing, I am saved.
Oh Father, help my unbelief, there is no other way.

> ..."When the spirit saw Jesus, it immediately threw the boy into a convulsion. He fell to the ground and rolled around, foaming at the mouth. Jesus asked the boy's father, "How long has he been like this?" "From childhood," he answered. "It has often thrown him into fire or water to kill him. But if you can do anything, take pity on us and help us." "'If you can'?" said Jesus. "Everything is possible for him who believes." Immediately the boy's father exclaimed, "I do believe; help me overcome my unbelief!" (Mark 9:20-24 NIV)

Now Is The Time! – Fish and Bread Revisited

In the story of the feeding of the 5000, Jesus accepts a boy's lunch, blesses it, and distributes it to the people in attendance. Not only does everyone eat their fill but they gather up 12 large baskets full of leftovers. How many people would have gone hungry that day if a boy had not stepped up and offered to share his lunch? How many people would have died in their sins, if Christ, "the bread of life" had not stepped up to offer His body as a sacrifice for sin?

I don't pretend to understand it all, but I believe that this man they call Jesus is the embodiment of God himself, love incarnate, the salvation of the whole world. It begins and ends with the Christ!

As my 7-year-old explained it to me at the time, "God is Jesus and Jesus is God." Through Him all things were made and through Him all things are redeemed. I don't know if you can accept that or not, but I believe it is true. And I believe that *"now is the time of God's favor, now is the day of salvation." (2 Corinthians 6:2 NIV). 'Today, if you hear his voice, do not harden your hearts." (Hebrews 3:15 NIV)* but believe and act on that belief!

It is not my intent to guilt or to scare you into accepting something that you cannot readily confess. What you believe is what you believe, and you can only believe what has been given to you to believe. If you believe, as I do that Jesus is the Christ, then act on it! If you believe in kindness, or goodness, or mercy, or forgiveness, or love, then act on those things.

For I suspect, that if you share any of those things with another, *"'you are not far from the kingdom of God.'" (Mark 12:34 NIV)* And Jesus said, *"...if anyone gives even a cup of cold water to one of these little ones who is my disciple, truly I tell you, that person will certainly not lose their reward." (Matthew 10:42 NIV)* So at the risk of taking undue liberty with the scripture and tumbling headlong into heresy, I would suggest that just perhaps there is more faith in God, in one small act of love than in all the words and creeds ever written.

If on the other hand, you believe in hurting or harming people and doing unto others before they do it unto you; if you believe in harboring grudges or unforgiveness or hatred in your heart; if you distrust God's motives or believe he doesn't even exist, then cut it out! Let God turn you around! Then go in the other direction! You do not want to cross God! Quite simply, He brought you into this world and He can take you out! But more importantly, you have a loving heavenly Father who wants nothing more than to give you good things and a brother Jesus who gave His very life for you that you might have life and have it abundantly! They promise to be with you, no matter how difficult things may get and to place the Holy Spirit within you! So, with all that going for you, why do you need to hurt or harm other people? You see *"This is love: not that we loved God, but that he loved us and sent his Son as an atoning sacrifice for our sins. Dear friends, since God so loved us, we also ought to love one another."*

(1 John 4:10-11 NIV) So turn around, "repent," believe and put that belief into action.

I am not proposing a salvation based on works and I am not trying to water down Jesus or the good news that He died and rose again so that we might have forgiveness of sins and everlasting life. Indeed, with God's help and by His grace, I cling to this confession with all my heart and soul and it is my earnest prayer that God will give you this confession as well. But if not, act on the good that you do believe!

Who is to say what will be the outcome! Now is the time to put belief into action! Today is the only NOW we have! Don't put off doing the good you can do today. Tomorrow may never come! Offer up your fish and bread! You will not go hungry! For who knows the results of one small act of kindness and the salvation and good it may bring to the giver or the receiver. Who knows the miracles which will be performed by the Master's hands or how He will multiply our gifts! For love, indeed, *"covers over a multitude of sins" (1 Peter 4:8 NIV),* and if as the apostle John says, *"God is Love!" (1 John 4:8 & 16 NIV),* then perhaps, just perhaps, there is hope for all of us. Not because of what we do, but because of God's amazing grace in Christ Jesus.

So, I say shun evil and *"cling to what is good" (Romans 12:9 NIV)* and if you have any faith in goodness, any belief in God or any inkling that Jesus might be the Christ, then as your faith allows, make this your confession and prayer:

Father, source of all goodness and love, I do believe! Help my unbelief and turn my faith into action! My actions into blessings for many! May it be so!

In Jesus Name.

> *...How then can we be saved? All of us have become like one who is unclean, and all our righteous acts are like filthy rags; we all shrivel up like a leaf, and like the wind our sins sweep us away. No one calls on your name or strives to lay hold of you; for you have hidden your face from us and have given us over to our sins. Yet*

you, Lord, are our Father. We are the clay, you are the potter; we are all the work of your hand. Do not be angry beyond measure, Lord; do not remember our sins forever. Oh, look on us, we pray, for we are all your people. (Isaiah 64:5-9 NIV)

So, I find this law at work: Although I want to do good, evil is right there with me. For in my inner being I delight in God's law; but I see another law at work in me, waging war against the law of my mind and making me a prisoner of the law of sin at work within me. What a wretched man I am! Who will rescue me from this body that is subject to death? Thanks be to God, who delivers me through Jesus Christ our Lord! (Romans 7:21-25 NIV)

To ponder, journal and/or perhaps share:

1. Remember a time when someone blessed you with an act of kindness, love, forgiveness, or mercy.

2. Recall a time you reached out in kindness, love, forgiveness, or mercy.

3. What event or person has helped to make God's kindness, love, forgiveness, or mercy real to you?

4. What words if any stick with you from the writings above? What feelings do these words above evoke in you?

5. Is the sound of the drum and trumpet calling you to battle or surrender? Why?

6. What is one area of your life in which you still need to seek "terms of peace" with God?

7. The author seems to think that faith, belief is a gift? What do you think about that?

8. What is one area of unbelief or doubt that you need help with?

9. What is one act of kindness that you can do today?

10. What "charge" would you like to lead? What "lunch" would you like to share?

11. What is another question that the writings above cause you to ask?

Created with a Pixabay Image from ArtsyBee

Created with a Pixabay Image from PublicDomainPictures

Image created with PicSay Pro by Karlie

Chapter Four

Snapshots from the Family Album

"Children's children are a crown to the aged, and parents are the pride of their children. ... A friend loves at all times, and a brother is born for a time of adversity." (Proverbs 17: 6, 17 NIV)

I was born into a family with a mom, a dad, and three older sisters. A fourth sister, Susan had been stillborn. My younger brother joined the clan just over a year later and so the semi-organized chaos we called our family was complete. Growing up, I took my family for granted. It was just an ordinary family and it would be many years before I would recognize just how extraordinary my family truly was.

My first recollection that my parents and family might be different than others, occurred in Jr. High when a science teacher, who had me and at least some of my sisters in class, commented that my parents "must really do something right." I had no idea what that something was, but it did make me stop and think for a moment that maybe my parents were alright after all.

We were not a perfect family by any means. Our house was often messy, probably because, my parents, Ralph (R.B.) and Alberta (Bert) both worked, (no doubt to make ends meet). I don't ever remember my parents saying, "I love you," when we were growing up and hugs were reserved for visits to grandma's. I guess when I stopped to consider it, I knew they loved me. In retrospect I think they did the best they could and that was more than good enough!

My dad was a big man, with a big voice and an erratic temper. Things would seem to be going along just fine and then he would explode, yelling and raging and sending everyone either scrambling into action or for a place to hide. I suspect the volatility and unpredictability of these actions overshadowed things and made it seem like these angry eruptions happened more frequently than they did. He used to joke that he was the most even-tempered man around, "mad all the time." While simply not true, it sometimes felt that way. I remember the yelling made me feel small, perhaps I wanted to disappear. Likewise, the threat of a spanking "with the belt" was held over our heads, often creating an atmosphere of uncertainty and fear.

In fairness, (and maybe my brother and sisters remember it differently) I don't ever remember getting a spanking either with or without a belt. My dad did clunk my brother's and my head together on one occasion, when we really got into it. Not a parenting technique I recommend, but it was very effective at the time.

My dad was in many ways a great dad with many redeeming qualities. There were many good times with my dad, and he taught me many things, but the fear I had of him, the feelings that I could never fully please him, and the inconsistency of his anger made it difficult to feel close to him. Only in adulthood did that fear, and those feelings completely disappear. Only after being a father myself did I gain a renewed appreciation for my dad and the difficulties of life and parenting. Only in processing and dealing with my own shortcomings could I begin to understand and forgive my dad's shortcomings and let go of and begin to heal from the largely unintentional hurt his actions may have caused.

My mom, in her own perhaps codependent way, was the mediator in the family. She would settle arguments among us kids and intercede for us when my dad's anger appeared to be getting out of hand. She held things together, all while either working a job or helping in one of my dad's many businesses or sometimes both. She has a tremendous capacity to love! Though not perfect, she is an amazing woman, who grows more amazing with each passing day!

My brother Steve, I remember as a skinny little kid with a temper. At any rate, we fought, as brothers often do (of course, he always started it). Yet, he was also my best friend growing up. Together we explored Brook Dell Park, Potter's Lake, and many points beyond and in between. He was more adventurous and outgoing than I. So, while he was younger, he often forged the trail.

I will always remember the day I returned home from college to find that my "scrawny little brother," was now something over 6 feet tall, with broad shoulders and bulging muscles. Though we hadn't fought in years, there was still the horrible realization that I could no longer take him.

My sister, Judy, was the closest sister to me in age, only two years older. She was my favorite sister growing up, but there was that fateful morning when we were walking to school and the warning bell rang. She broke into a run and jumped a ditch, an easy feat for a second-grader, not so easy for a kindergartener. My foot caught the edge of the ditch and I went down face first in the mud. I was covered in slime, and she left me to return home alone to change.

My sister, Debbie was three years older. I don't have many early memories of her, but at least I don't remember her as being mean, so I guess she was alright! I remember once she got her hair cut short and I liked it. I remember when she was in high school and started dating Jim, Steve and I were the epitome of annoying little brothers. I remember we stole him away one night to go riding motorcycle trails in his sports car, sandwiched in with a trip from one turnpike exit to the next, at speeds that were other than legal.

Then there was Nancy, seven years my elder, she was often called on to babysit. The first picture that came to mind, was of her talking to a friend on the phone about some strange thing called "algebra" with "variables" and things like a + b = c. My second memory is of the day she grabbed me by the arm separating bone from flesh. I guess for the most part she was alright, as big sisters go. I looked up to her with a sense of awe and wonder.

So, what about me? I remember myself as a quiet kid, kind of shy. I was smart, but I don't think I realized it until I was in High School. I was born with a deformed left arm, a "clubbed hand," but my parents and my brother and sisters never let me use it as an excuse to not try things. Consequently, I did most everything other kids do, and though occasionally self-conscious of my arm, (I remember I went through a stage where I would only wear long sleeve shirts.) usually I and others never gave it a second thought. I was a thinker and a daydreamer, and I loved to pretend. I was content just being me.

That is a short and rather oversimplified snapshot of my family of origin. How my mom and dad ever managed with five kids, I'll never know. The clan these days has grown significantly with the addition of grandchildren, great-grandchildren, great-great-grandchildren, and in-laws of all types. My dad died over 20 years ago, and though my mom, now 92, shows a few signs of slowing down, she remains active and involved with her family. In some ways my family is close, in other ways were not. Scattered about the country, we get together when we can and when we do, each is genuinely interested in how the others are doing. We love each other (it's easier now that we don't live together) and we are getting better at saying it. There are rarely disagreements and I hope what's written here does not spark any, but that it pulls us even closer together. My 7th-grade science teacher was right, despite their imperfections, "my parents must have really done something right." We are not and never were the perfect family, but stacked up against the turmoil, I have seen in so many families, we have much to be thankful for. I love you guys!

Strength & Beauty (Ode to Ralph and Alberta)

They tread the mountains and roam the valleys without fear,
For he is the biggest buck, she the most graceful doe,
But whether by muzzle flash or simply in the passing of the years,
Even the biggest buck and the most graceful doe learn,
What the fawn already knows,
That their lives are held within the creator's hand.

The Bull of the Woods is Dead (In Memory of Dad)

The bull of the woods is dead,
His passing came without much to do,
Holed up in a thicket to stay out of the wind and snow.
In his younger days, he bellowed and bugled, backing up every challenge,
But as the years passed, he found, that often a bluff would do.
When that strategy failed him, he only bellowed, when there were no challengers around.
Though often loud, proud and boisterous,
He came to know his place,
And so, he passed quite silently, enfolded in God's grace.

Little Boy Lost

Lord, I was a little one once, beloved in my Father's eyes.
Nothing upset me then - nor was I shy.
I gladly went about my life, not afraid to try.
Not afraid to laugh or cry, too naive to lie.
I must have told You everything,
For whom else could understand.
Whatever happened to that little child?
Alas, I fear, he became a man.

Legacy of the Wolf

Get that "R" off of there!
I want nothing to do with that ravenous wolf!
My child, My child, don't you know,
That wolf is your mother and your kind father!
Don't you know that wolf is you!
You are what you are, and I love you anyway!
And I can make all things new!

Wolf Child

God looked down from heaven above on a child,
So battered and bruised,
That many said the child would not survive,
But he did.

God looked down on a man,
So hardened by the years,
That some said nothing could break through,
But You did.

God looked down on a hopeless case, a self-devouring wolf.
They said, "The beast must be destroyed!"
But God said, "Not yet, not yet."

God looked down on one for whom He had died and said,
"My grace is sufficient, my precious, precious child."
And then He sent me on my way!

The Ghosts of My Childhood

Casper "the friendly ghost"
You pulled his string and he would talk and sing!

A childhood toy given to me, at age three,
Along with a book about fire trucks.
Given to soothe me before and after surgery,
A traumatic event, with its own gift of "not so friendly ghosts",
Ghosts of fear, anxiety, and feelings of abandonment!
Casper "the friendly ghost",
You pulled his string and he would talk and sing

My Fathers Tears

Tears well up in my eyes, from time to time,
Sometimes they flow openly,
They are my father's tears.
I inherited them from him.
I cry easier than he,
He was a harder man than I,
It took more to move him,
But I saw those tears, on occasion
In the corners of his eyes…
Perhaps a movie - a photo – a memory - a funeral -
the kindness or pain of a child - or of my mom…
Released them.
Not often, not flowing, but tears!
I inherited my father's tears,
A significant part of his growing legacy,
As I process the pain and joy,
As I learn from both his successes and his shortcomings.
I cry easier than he.
But they are my Father's tears

In the Presence of the Accuser

I burst into poetry, I burst into song,
To my loving Father, my strength to go on.

You have loved me through the years with Your unrelenting love,
Watching, working, wrangling from Your heavenly home above.

In the person of Your Son, I find the power to forgive,
All the evil people, who would inside me live.
Demons far too numerous to name them one by one,
Fathers, mothers, sisters, rebellious, unforgiving sons!

The words I write are mystery, fact or fantasy, I'm not sure,
But of this you can be certain, Jesus is the cure!
Hold on to Him with all your might,
When you're tested and you're tried,
For sooner or later, the judgment will arrive!
Then when accosted by that accuser, that liar and that thief,
Lean but on these simple words, "Jesus died for me!"

But My Family Sucks!

So, what if your family or your life in general is/was even less perfect than mine? What if it is/was indeed terrible? What if family members or others have violated and defiled your boundaries of body, mind, and spirit and have hurt you beyond measure? My first, very much less than professional, overly simple, no-right-to-give-it, and definitely-not-easy answer to those questions is to forgive. And while there is much truth in that prescription to forgive, the process of healing from the hurt and harm others have intentionally or unintentionally caused, or even healing from and dealing with the hurts, sorrows and difficulties inflicted by the seeming randomness of life, in general, is often not that simple. It is a process with perhaps as many questions as answers.

Questions such as: Do I want to heal? How do I heal? Do I want to forgive? Is it helpful to forgive? How do I forgive without condoning the actions perpetrated against me? What traumas, big and little have I experienced and what hold do they have on me today? Do I want to let go of anger, sorrow, pain, disappointment, betrayal, abandonment, despair, fear, anxiety, blame, hate, and a host of other feelings and emotions and is it even possible to let go of these things? Am I willing to be honest with myself and others? Will it help? What feelings am I hiding, repressing, or burying so that I don't have to deal with them? What relationships do I want to preserve and what ones do I need to let go of? What do I need to understand about or accept or forgive in myself or others that will enable me to heal and progress? How do my perceptions of things affect my reality? Do I have patterns of thinking or negative beliefs that are holding me back? Do I blame others for my troubles? Do I blame God for my troubles? Indeed, why would God let these things happen to me? Does blame help me or hurt me? Am I happy with the way things are? Do I want to change? Do I need to change? How do I change? Do I really want or need to dig up or revisit old hurts? Is it worth it? Do I need professional help? Where do I begin? How do I begin? What Is the first step or the next step?

The process can seem overwhelming, and **the journey to survive and thrive, the journey toward healing, wholeness, wellbeing, peace, joy, and acceptance can be long, even lifelong. In my opinion, it is a journey worth taking, and while it is an individual journey, again in my opinion, it is not one you should take alone. So, what is the first step or the next step on this journey?**

It might be to seek out a good counselor, trusted friend, or support group with whom to share some of your thoughts and feelings. (Remember don't make the journey alone!) It might be to put pen to paper or finger to keyboard and honestly answer some of the questions above or alternately to sit down and "free write" whatever comes to mind without pausing to question or judge. It might be to read a book or watch a video on a topic such as trauma, healing, or forgiveness. It might be to open a dialog with God through prayer, meditation, or journaling. It might be to clip out words and/or pictures from magazines and make a collage of your thoughts and feelings, or to create a drawing or painting. It might be to sit and quietly reflect. It might be that you forgive someone or yourself. It might be to cry some tears or call a friend or both? **It might be one of hundreds of things, the important thing is that as you are willing and able, with God's help, take the next step!**

Father,

Show me the next step and give me the courage and strength to take it. Go with me and lead me and give me faithful and helpful traveling companions in this journey of forgiveness, recovery, and healing.

In Jesus Name. Amen!

Cast all your anxiety on him because he cares for you. (1 Peter 5:7 NIV)

To ponder, journal and/or perhaps share:

1. Is your memory of your family growing up primarily positive or negative? Why? What is the most prominent memory of your mother? Of your Father? Of Your brothers and sisters?

2. What is your favorite memory growing up?

3. Who is your favorite family member? Why?

4. Recall a time when you got in trouble as a child? How did the adults react? What, if anything, would you have wished they did instead?

5. Is there a characteristic, habit (positive or negative), or something you do, that you have "inherited" from your Father or Mother? What?

6. Has your family helped or hindered your view of God and your relationship with Him? Why is that?

7. Who or what in your life has hurt you the most? How do you feel about that person, thing, or event now?

8. Who or what in your life brings you happiness or joy? Why?

9. The Bible tells us in many places to forgive others. What do you think about that? How easy is it for you to forgive? Is there anyone you have not forgiven? Why is that? What do you need from God to heal from your hurt? What do you need from God to forgive those who hurt you? What boundaries do you need to establish to protect yourself or others? What help do you need from others in all this? Is forgiveness more of a decision or an emotion/feeling? Is forgiveness more for you or those who hurt you? Have you ever thought of praying, "I do forgive, help my unforgiveness!" What is one thing you can do right now to grow in the area of forgiveness?

10. What might be the next step on your journey toward healing and wholeness? Are you willing to take it?

Image created by Karlie

Created with a Pixabay Image from PublicDomainPictures

Chapter Five

From "I do!"
to
"Been There and Done That!"

"A wife of noble character who can find? She is worth far more than rubies... Her children arise and call her blessed; her husband also, and he praises her:" (Proverbs 31:10, 28)

Psychologists and behavioral scientists often emphasize the family in which we grew up and its impact on our development, but of all the people I'm related to, none have had a more profound effect on me than my wife and children. They have taught me more about life, love, faith, forgiveness, encouragement, and hundreds of other things, than I could ever put into words.

My wife, Linda, and I met in college. We were both transfer students, and though we knew each other for over a year, it wasn't until we started student teaching that we really got to know each other. We were among a group of student teachers who had breakfast together each morning, long before most other students were getting up. Well, one thing led to another, as they say, and we began to see more and more of each other. A year and a half later we were married. Forty years, two daughters, many hard times, and even more good times later, I am beginning to know what love is all about.

We've been there, done that, and are doing it again, but this time as grandparents. So far, we've added a son-in-law, Kevin and granddaughters, Karlie and Maddie to the mix. As we see our children (Kevin we include you there) and grandchildren grow and struggle, learn and laugh, the memories of our own family flood back and faith, hope, and love are born anew.

Linda's Love

Linda's Love is an enduring love,
A lip-biting, look-the-other-way love.
Linda's love is a life-giving, living love,
A lavish, lucid, lingering love.
Linda's love is a ludicrous love,
A long-suffering, life-sustaining, languishing love.
Linda's love is an imperfect love,
A sometimes, unhealthy love,
But Linda's love is an enduring love.
And I love her.

A Child's Love

There once was a man so hardened by the years,
That they said his heart was stone.
A stone so hard it could not be broken,
At least those were the words that were spoken.
But then there came a child,
And love in words and actions spoken,
And though the stone could not be broken,
Love's fire began to melt it

Precious Gifts

My wife and daughters,
Are such precious gifts!
Bringing me God's love

> *A wife of noble character who can find? She is worth far more than rubies. Her husband has full confidence in her and lacks nothing of value. She brings him good, not harm, all the days of her life. (Proverbs 31:10-12 NIV)*

> *Children are a heritage from the Lord, offspring a reward from him. Like arrows in the hands of a warrior are children born in one's youth. Blessed is the man whose quiver is full of them. They will not be put to shame… (Psalm 127:3-5 NIV)*

Tornado Child

crayons, and coloring things
bubble blowers and princess or pirate rings
squirt guns, 5-mile runs,
in the backyard
on the stairway
the park, around the block,
with a friend
all alone
skinned knees
dirty shirt
mud pies
trouble
sleep
… whatever you do, do it all for the glory of God.
(1 Corinthians 10:31 NIV)

Giraffe Cookies at 5:00 am

I was sitting typing quietly when I heard my daughter cry.
I went to see, what was the matter, and this was her reply,
"I want my cookie!" she said amidst her dreams.
I offered to get it. "No, I want my mommy!"
So, I carried her to mommy, now awakened by the wail,
But, alas, this action also, was to no avail.
For no sooner, had I delivered her to her mother's waiting arms,
Then she increased the wailing's volume,
Again, sounding this alarm,
"I want my cookie!" She said it, time and time.
I got one from the kitchen, then came this little rhyme,
"Not that one, the giraffe one!" cried the little voice.
I said, "You're dreaming honey,"
But the giraffe was still her choice!
So, back to the kitchen, this time with her in tow.
We searched all the cabinets. We searched both high and low.
I knew we wouldn't find any giraffes hiding there,
But to pacify my two-year-old, we searched everywhere.
She wanted to trust me, but she had to see it for herself.
She wasn't quite convinced,
There were no giraffes upon our shelf.
Now awake and half-contented,
She made a more reasonable demand,
"Red juice in a ducky-cup!" Her wish was my command!

There's a lesson here in all of this, to me it's very plain.
For often have I come to God, with requests quite insane!
Oh, they seemed so very reasonable, to me, at the time,
When in fact, they were more far-fetched,
Then the ones within this rhyme.
But God, listened and He searched with me,
And though giraffes I had in mind,
Red juice and a ducky-cup will be just more than fine.

...who satisfies your desires with good things so that your youth is renewed like the eagle's. (Psalm 103:5 NIV)

Victory

Father let me laugh in Satan's face,
And run like hell to heavens gates.
Let me know the life You give - joy and love and happiness,
Excitement and exhilaration - childlike things of expectation!
Let me play at heaven's door!
Enter in and leave no more!

> **'No, in all these things -we are more than conquerors through him who loved us. For I am convinced that neither death nor life, neither angels nor demons, neither the present nor the future, nor any powers, neither height nor depth, nor anything else in all creation, will be able to separate us from the love of God that is in Christ Jesus our Lord. " (Romans 8:37-39 NIV)**

When I Grow Up

When I grow up, I want to be a fireman and a forest ranger,
A big-game hunter and a fishing guide,
A teacher and a pastor,
A CPA and a PhD.
When I grow up, I want to be a lawyer and a doctor,
A scientist and a computer expert.
I want to build houses and raise cattle and crops!
I'll play baseball and tennis!
When I grow up, I'll be an entrepreneur,
And I'll work for somebody else!
I'll make lots of money and help all the poor people!
When I grow up, I want to be me!
Do you suppose they pay people for that?
Maybe they will, by the time I grow up!

The Return of the Giraffe Cookies

...and then sometime later,
My daughter came to me with shouts of glee!
"Look, daddy! Here are my giraffe cookies!"
She said, clutching a strangled box of animal crackers -
Retrieved from who knows where.
"Look here's a giraffe!"
She said, as she unceremoniously bit his head off!
And it was as if God laughed and whispered in my ear
"Giraffe cookies go great with red juice in a ducky-cup!"

> **Take delight in the Lord, and he will give you the desires of your heart. (Psalm 37:4 NIV)**

Daddy God

I'm a little one, trying hard to grow, trying... trying so -You know? You know, don't You, Lord? It's no ploy -Not meant to deliberately annoy.
Please, Mr. God, Please, daddy God, tell me the story again, about how we'll win -
About what it's like in heaven, about a world without any sin.
Oh, how we'll sing, what anthems will ring. Please daddy, tell us the story again!

> **And I heard a loud voice from the throne saying, "Look! God's dwelling place is now among the people, and he will dwell with them. They will be his people, and God himself will be with them and be their God. 'He will wipe every tear from their eyes. There will be no more death or mourning or crying or pain, for the old order of things has passed away." He who was seated on the throne said, "I am making everything new!"... (Revelation 21:3-5 NIV)**

Aftermath of a Snow Day at Papa's (with Morning and Evening assists from Grandma)

In the family room, the fuzzy, blue blanket hangs limply over the elliptical machine; a paint-marred-chair sits strategically nearby; remnants of Karlie's makeshift tent, constructed sometime amidst the evening's festivities and feuds, involving tired grandkids, toys, Olympics, an iPad and "stuff." Liberally, though not always randomly, dispersed throughout the room, are blocks, baby dolls, barbies, and blankets. Puzzles, a toy castle, doll stroller, Maddie's play tent, assorted figurines, a stuffed monkey, and papa's recliner, round out the picture. Also, a paper bowl, which once, precariously and somewhat successfully, constrained penguin crackers from being strewn here and there; now, rests peacefully on the little yellow table! And we mustn't forget, the iPad, the Android tablet, Kindle Fire, a phone and a laptop recharging from what was certainly a day of technology overuse and abuse; but which, gratefully, produced moments of calm and retreat, amidst the previous day's creative chaos.

Grandma's sewing and craft room, from which the chair was retrieved, is likewise, somewhat disarrayed. Scraps of paper on the floor, smudges on the table, and markers, paints and crayons, yet to be put away, provide evidence of the morning's art session; though the actual projects have been spirited away; to be shared with mom, dad, neighbors and friends or if stamps and envelopes can be found, sent to Aunt Bekah in Buffalo!

Upstairs, in the kitchen, the empty pizza box and Kool-aide pitcher, along with discarded cheese wrappers, paper plates, and sandwich crusts, indicate, that though nutrition may have been lacking, the little ones were at least fed.

The living room, furniture still pushed to the walls, (necessary, of course, to clear space for cartwheels, somersaults, and all forms of gymnastics and dance) has a new, open and expansive feel! A plastic Joseph, never put away from Christmas, peeks out from under one of the couch cushions, vigilantly watching and observing! Left there, when a game of "hide-them-and-come-find-them" was suddenly interrupted, for something more enticing; he and his perhaps-never-to-be-discovered, manger-scene companions, lurk hidden, in the yet-dark, morning stillness.

In that stillness, Grandma sleeps, enjoying some much-deserved rest, before heading off to teach school! And Papa, up early, to write, reflect and begin the clean-up; smiles and give thanks!

> ***Rejoice always, pray continually, give thanks in all circumstances; for this is God's will for you in Christ Jesus.***
> ***(1 Thessalonians 5:16-18 NIV)***
>
> ***Children's children are a crown to the aged, and parents are the pride of their children. (Proverbs 17:6 NIV)***

<u>A Father's Love</u>

Father, if that is the name by which You will be called,
Then I know You love me,
For I am a father too and I love my children.
Look down on me, oh my God and Father,
Let us not provoke each other to anger,
But work and laugh and play with each other,
Cooperating to make each other's life...
Full of joy and complete.
Perhaps it is foolish to think that I could add anything to Your day,
But I know how much my children add to mine.
I know how much they teach me.
They bring me from the arrogant adolescence of theology,
To the humble adulthood of love and childlike faith.
I love You, Dad!

> *See what great love the Father has lavished on us, that we should be called children of God! And that is what we are! (1 John 3:1 NIV)*
>
> *If you, then, though you are evil, know how to give good gifts to your children, how much more will your Father in heaven give good gifts to those who ask him! (Matthew 7:11 NIV)*

Just One More Story, Daddy

Just one more, daddy?
Please! Please, just one more,
Tell us one about the angels!
We want to hear about the angels!
My precious child, you have already entertained angels unaware,
Now go in peace.
But daddy, we want to learn about the angels!
Please, please, tell us the one about the angels!
Please, please, show us the angels, please!
Oh, alright! Here they come!
Z-o-o-o-m! Beep, Beep! I got one!
You didn't get one; you're tickling me!
Yes, I know my child. Yes, I know -
Now go in peace, you have a message to bring!

> *The wolf will live with the lamb, the leopard will lie down with the goat, the calf and the lion and the yearling together; and a little child will lead them. The cow will feed with the bear, their young will lie down together, and the lion will eat straw like the ox. The infant will play near the cobra's den, and the young child will put its hand into the viper's nest. They will neither harm nor destroy on all my holy mountain, for the earth will be filled with the knowledge of the Lord as the waters cover the sea. (Isaiah 11:6-9 NIV)*
>
> *Keep on loving one another as brothers and sisters. Do not forget to show hospitality to strangers, for by so doing some people have shown hospitality to angels without knowing it.*
> *(Hebrews 13:1-2 NIV)*

Let Your Light Shine

Enough, enough my child, you can't go on!
Go to bed and wake up dead, to sin and evil folly.
Trust in God! Obey His rod and be so jolly,
That the whole world sees and emulates,
The "I in you" and "you in Me!"

> **In the same way, let your light shine before others, that they may see your good deeds and glorify your Father in heaven. (Matthew 5:16 NIV)**

To ponder, journal and/or perhaps share:

1. What are three words that describe your family now?

2. Is there a person (or persons) who has made the meaning of love (or God's love) real to you? Who was that person? What did they do or say?

3. What were three things you enjoyed doing as a child? When was the last time you did them?

4. When you were a child, what did you want to be when you grew up?

5. What's one of the most far-fetched things you ever asked God or someone else for?

6. What's one of the most amazing or outrageous things you ever received from God or someone else?

7. Of the poems and passages in this chapter, which one is most meaningful to you? Why?

8. How do you picture heaven? How does your picture of heaven differ (if at all) from the picture you had as a child?

9. What are three words that described you as a child? What are three words that describe you now? What child-like characteristic would you most like to regain?

10. Recall a time that you were so excited that you could not sleep.

11. What message has God given you to bring to the world? How or with whom, would you most like to share it?

12. Recall a time when your light shined.

13. What is one area of your life in which you would like God's help to be victorious? What would victory look like? Feel Like?

Created with a Pixabay Image from GDJ

Created with a Pixabay Image from johnhain

Chapter Six

Reflections of Relentless Love

"The Lord appeared to us in the past, saying: "I have loved you with an everlasting love; I have drawn you with unfailing kindness. I will build you up again, ..." (Jeremiah 31:3-4a)

"For the Lord is good and his love endures forever: his faithfulness continues through all generations." (Psalm 100:5)

I love John Godfrey Saxe's version of the famous Indian legend, of the blind men and an elephant.

The Blind Men and the Elephant
by John Godfrey Saxe (Public Domain.)

It was six men of Indostan
To learning much inclined,
Who went to see the Elephant
(Though all of them were blind),
That each by observation
Might satisfy his mind.

The First approached the Elephant,
And happening to fall

Against his broad and sturdy side,
At once began to bawl:
"God bless me! but the Elephant Is very like a wall!"

The Second, feeling of the tusk,
Cried, -"Ho! what have we here
So very round and smooth and sharp?
To me 'tis mighty clear
This wonder of an Elephant Is very like a spear!"

The Third approached the animal,
And happening to take
The squirming trunk within his hands,
Thus boldly up and spake:
"I see," quoth he, "the Elephant Is very like a snake!"

The Fourth reached out his eager hand,
And felt about the knee.
"What most this wondrous beast is like
Is mighty plain," quoth he,
"'Tis clear enough the Elephant Is very like a tree!"

The Fifth, who chanced to touch the ear,
Said: "E'en the blindest man
Can tell what this resembles most;
Deny the fact who can,
This marvel of an Elephant Is very like a fan!"

The Sixth no sooner had begun
About the beast to grope,
Then, seizing on the swinging tail
That fell within his scope,
"I see," quoth he, "the Elephant Is very like a rope!"

And so these men of Indostan

Disputed loud and long,
Each in his own opinion
Exceeding stiff and strong,
Though each was partly in the right,
And all were in the wrong!

MORAL.
So oft in theologic wars,
The disputants, I ween,
Rail on in utter ignorance
Of what each other mean,
And prate about an Elephant
Not one of them has seen!

All of us have "blind spots," areas of our lives, or in our belief systems, in which we are blind and cannot appreciate the thoughts or beliefs of others. We cling to either-or thinking and cannot embrace the idea that the true picture might be a both-and or something other than what we believe. I am, probably, no less blind than others. I paint a picture of God based upon the part of the whole that has been revealed to me. That part to a large extent is love! To me, it defines the essence and activity of God!

I cling to a traditional interpretation of the Bible and Christianity (though some would probably dispute that), but I must confess that sometimes my spirit or perhaps my ego rightly or wrongly cries out for something far beyond tradition. Perhaps it is not so much the traditional teachings that it rails against as much as the intolerance and even violence with which they have been defended and derailed. When I think of the sins and atrocities that have been committed throughout history in the name of Jesus, I weep! Yet, much good has been done in that strong name as well. So, I cling to the traditions and teachings of our church, but I must also allow for the possibility that, in our humanness and sinfulness, in our stubbornness and limited ability to understand, we may have it all wrong.

The more I studied scripture and tried to understand God, the more I realized how little we can know for certain. As I mentioned before, I drove myself mad trying to build a box big enough to contain it all. Now, most days anyway, I am content to live in God's grace and mercy. Content to let God be God and "me" be me. Content to do my best with God's help to love, forgive and accept others, even or perhaps especially when they do not agree with me or their actions do not reciprocate in kind.

"For God so loved the world that He sent His only begotten Son, that whosoever believes in Him, should not perish, but have eternal life." "This is love: not that we loved God, but that He loved us and sent His Son as the propitiation for our sins, friends, since God so loved us, we ought also to love one another." "No one has ever seen God; but if we love one another, God lives in us and His love is made perfect in us." "This is my commandment that you love one another!" "Love one another as I have loved you!" "Greater love hath no one than to lay down his life for his friends!" "By this they will know that you are my disciples, if you love one another." "Love Your Enemies!" "Love the Lord your God with all your heart, and with all your soul, with all your strength and with all your mind, and your neighbor as yourself." "GOD IS LOVE!"

Excuse me if these are not perfect quotes, but there is a theme here, a theme that God is relentless in His love for us and that we should be relentless in our love for one another. It's one of those "simple, but not easy" kinds of things. It is not easy to at times to know what is the most loving action to take; to know how to love the sinner without condoning the sin; how to disagree without being disagreeable; or even to know sometimes whether something is right or wrong, fair or just or merciful, helpful or loving.

It's even more difficult when played out on a national or international level. For example, is it right to use violence as a means to combat violence, injustice or tyranny? I certainly don't have all the answers, or even all the questions, but too often we give up trying. We must be relentless in our motivation and efforts to love one another. We must keep listening and talking and listening and loving. We must examine our actions and ask if they are motivated by love!

It's difficult to know where to even start, but perhaps we start by speaking or at least thinking the words, "I love you!" In my own family these three simple words, "I love you!" have had a profound impact. We had an unwritten rule that my wife and I would speak these words to each other and to our children every day. We probably missed a day here or there, but not many. Perhaps these words would have been hollow if they had not been backed up by action, but there were many times such as disagreements, tough teen years and my periods of depression, when these words reassured each other that the underlying relationship of care and concern was still intact, even if at the time we disagreed, felt unloving or unlovable.

Perhaps speaking or thinking these words is too simple of a solution to work in other settings, perhaps not. What a difference it might make if we approached every person with the attitude that we love them. What a difference it might make if we looked at every person as a dearly loved child of God, as a person for whom Christ died, as a beloved brother or sister! Wouldn't this mind shift cause us to behave in more loving ways and to seek greater understanding and peace with those around us?

"I love you!" three simple words God speaks to us and demonstrates to us daily, if we are open to see and hear! If we are open to that love and willing to take this attitude toward others; if we are brave enough to speak and demonstrate these words to those around us; just maybe in little ways and even big it may begin to make a profound difference in our lives and the lives of others!

God loves you! I love you! Pass it on!

Love is patient, love is kind. It does not envy, it does not boast, it is not proud. It does not dishonor others, it is not self-seeking, it is not easily angered, it keeps no record of wrongs. Love does not delight in evil but rejoices with the truth. It always protects, always trusts, always hopes, always perseveres. Love never fails…
(1 Corinthians 13:4-8 NIV)

Whoever claims to love God yet hates a brother or sister is a liar. For whoever does not love their brother and sister, whom they have seen, cannot love God, whom they have not seen. And he has given us this command: Anyone who loves God must also love their brother and sister. (1 John 4:20-21 NIV)

Relentless, Everlasting Love

Oh, Father, words cannot express my gratitude to thee,
For healings far too wonderful, for paradox and mystery!
For though I tread the verge of destruction,
And though I walked the brim,
My good and gracious Father would not let me throw myself in.
He loves me with a relentless love!
He loves me! Loves me! Loves me!
He loves me with an everlasting love!
He has kept me through the night!
And why should this great wonder, be bestowed on such as me?
No reason, except you love me, all glory goes to Thee!

…"I have loved you with an everlasting love; I have drawn you with unfailing kindness. (Jeremiah 31:3 NIV)

This is love: not that we loved God, but that he loved us and sent his Son as an atoning sacrifice for our sins. Dear friends, since God so loved us, we also ought to love one another. No one has ever seen God; but if we love one another, God lives in us and his love is made complete in us. (1 John 4:10 -12 NIV)

This Thing Called Love

It is not often easy to love!
It is sometimes messy, this thing we call love!
Needy people surround us.
Call out to us.
Consume us!

It is not often easy to love!
But in it, there is often,
Much joy and great rejoicing,
And thanksgiving, and forgiveness,
And hope and praise!

It is messy business to love!
Filled with wonderful, awesome, messy people!
People corrupted by sin and evil!
People locked in a world of hopelessness and despair!

It is not easy to love!
But love we must!
For such is the good Spirit within us!
We mess it up and try again!
We get it all wrong sometimes,
And yet He, the Holy One, who is love itself,
Somehow, He works it all out for good!

It is not easy, this thing called love,
But we must love!
For at the core of our sin-wrecked lives is,
The seed of love!
The spark of love!

The Spirit of love!
And so, we must dive into the mess!
And do our best!
And pray for the Holy One to bless and multiply,
Our sometimes feeble and misguided efforts!

It is messy, this thing called love!
But fortunately,
God, our God, the source of love is not afraid!
Not afraid of getting his hands,
His whole body dirty!
He dives into the mess for our sake!
And He encourages us to do the same for others!

It is often messy, this thing called love!
But praise and thanks to the Father and to the Son,
Who pulls us out of the muck and mire!
Who washes us clean and clothes us in righteousness and love!
Who removes sin and death far from us!
And fills our hearts with songs of
Great rejoicing! Thanksgiving! And praise!

Dear Dyings

The night was dark,
The fawn stillborn,
And arms reach down to enfold one too precious to die.

The morn was bright, the air quite crisp,
The yearling danced to his death when the rocks gave way.
And arms reach down to enfold one too precious to die.

The sun was not too high, the dew not yet dry,

A bullet dropped the buck in mid-stride,
And arms reach down to enfold one too precious to die.

Afternoon came early, with a light rain,
The doe caught the scent too late; the wolves ripped her apart,
And arms reach down to enfold one too precious to die.

The evening was cold, white and silent,
The king of the woods lied down and never woke up.
And arms reach down to enfold one too precious to die.

The hunter was old and grey, worn out from many a long day,
But not so tired that he could not pray,
"Precious Father, receive me."
And arms reach down to enfold one too precious to die.

> **Are not two sparrows sold for a penny? Yet not one of them will fall to the ground outside your Father's care. And even the very hairs of your head are all numbered. So don't be afraid; you are worth more than many sparrows. (Matthew 10:29-31 NIV)**

Circle of Love

Oh God, be gracious to us. Look down on us we pray.
How fragile our existence, yet wonderfully, are we made.
Oh God, Most Holy God, hear us for Your own namesake.
Forgive us all our sins and grant to us a stake -
In Your eternal glory ... oh Mystery beyond all knowing,
Both here and in eternity, grant us wisdom, peace, and love;
Faith, hope, and fellowship with man and God above.

For in loving, there is hope, and in hope, encouragement.
And in fellowship with God and man, true life is forged and spent.

Goliath's Boast

*"I'm not afraid! You, **beep-beeps**, come out here and fight! You bunch of **beeps**! Drag your sorry **beeps** out here, if you've got any **beeps** at all! You think your sorry, **beep-beep** God can save you? Let me tell you something, your God ain't nothing but a **beep-beep-beep**. I'll tell you something else, 'Ye, though I walk through the valley of the shadow of death, I will fear no evil,' for I am the meanest **beep-beep** in the valley!" But then he met David, a servant of the living God, and with his last breath he whispered, "God of David, have mercy on me!" And his Father responded, "Let the party begin!"*

> ***I tell you that in the same way there will be more rejoicing in heaven over one sinner who repents than over ninety-nine righteous persons who do not need to repent. (Luke 15:7 NIV)***

Prophecy Revisited - The Seal is Broken

Tell them I love them! Tell them I care!
Tell them I will neither forsake them nor desert them!
Tell them that nothing can separate them from my love!
Tell them that when they cross over from that dark and distant country, not to listen to the voices of demons who would wrench babies from their mothers' arms!
Tell them to ignore their hideous faces, no matter how they may be disguised, no matter how enticing they may seem!
Tell them to cling tightly to their childhood memories of my affection, and to cry "Abba, Daddy, save me!"
Tell them to wrap themselves in the strong name of Jesus, and to speak it, even shout it with conviction and authority!
Tell them my Spirit goes before them like Elijah to prepare the way!
Tell them that when they come to their senses, they should run into the arms of their Father, who is running to meet them!
"...and when he was still a long way off, his father ran to him and embraced him and kissed him."

... "Do not fear, for I have redeemed you; I have summoned you by name; you are mine. When you pass through the waters, I will be with you; and when you pass through the rivers, they will not sweep over you. When you walk through the fire, you will not be burned; the flames will not set you ablaze. For I am the Lord your God, the Holy One of Israel, your Savior ... (Isaiah 43:1-3 NIV)

A Psalm of God's Relentless and Enduring Love

My soul yearns for You, even as my stomach churns in anguish and distress! My heart longs to be held by You! You are a God like no other, strong, yet loving and filled with tender mercy!

You hate sin, but You have an enduring and relentless love for sinners! You seek them out! You call them back! You run to embrace them! In my sin, I said, "Depart from me for I cannot stand in Your sight!" but You wrapped Your arms around me and clothed me with the robe of Your righteousness!

You did not overlook my sin but took it upon Yourself! You bore the burden of my shame! Therefore, I will praise Your Name! Because of Your great mercy and Your undying love, I am vindicated and will stand with the righteous! Though I sin a thousand times ten-thousand times, yet, You turn Your heart to me and forgive my transgressions! I am not worthy to be called by Your Name, but You have adopted me as Your son, made me Your precious child!

My soul yearns for You! Fill me with the gladness of Your good Spirit! It is good, Lord to be here! To experience all You have created! For even in the midst of so much evil, deception and sin, Your glory and Your goodness shine through!

Therefore, I will rejoice in Your creation! I will speak kindly to my brothers and sisters and not hold their shortcomings against them! I will proclaim to them Your marvelous deeds, Your great love and compassion and mercy!

You are a God who loves sinners and though You may destroy our bodies, yet our hope resides in You! My mind cannot comprehend Your ways or the joys You have in store for us! Therefore, in the midst of my distress, I will sing a song of joy! Out of the depths of my despair, shall alleluias resound!

If I had my way, I would live 111 years or perhaps 120 or even more and then be swept away by You, like Enoch or Elijah. But who am I to make such a request? Could I bear such length of days? Even if You renewed my strength, so that I was like a youth of twenty, could my soul endure the sorrows I would see?

Your ways are not my ways! Yours are far better! So even if my path is filled with pain and sorrow, even if I am led as one to the slaughter, yet by Your Good Spirit, which You set within me; will I trust in You! I have no faith of my own, no reason or strength to call my own, no courage, and no hope in myself! For all that I am and all that I have, You have given me! Your inheritance is light and love and life!

Therefore, I will instruct others in Your ways! Therefore, I will proclaim Your great goodness and mercy! If I go down to the depths, I will sing Your praise and if I rise up, I will shout, "Praise our God!"

Grant me humility and courage, good Father! Fill me with Your love that I might live this day well! My soul yearns for You!

To ponder, journal and/or perhaps share:

1. What are some of your "blind spots" when it comes to religious matters or people who believe differently than you?

2. Recall a time when you rushed to a conclusion before having all the evidence.

3. List one to five words that sum up God's essence for you.

4. What kind of people are the hardest for you to love?

5. Have you ever felt unloved or unlovable? When? Why?

6. What demons try to entice you away from God?

7. What would you fight and die for? What would you "lay down your life" for? Are the two the same? If not how are they different?

8. In your opinion which is more important hearing the words "I love you" or experiencing love in action? Why? Are both necessary?

9. What in this chapter, if anything, challenged your thinking about God or about love?

10. What person would you be most surprised to "see in heaven?" Why?

11. What does " living this day well," look like for you? What do you need from God to help you achieve that?

Created with a Pixabay Image from Clker-Free-Vector-Images

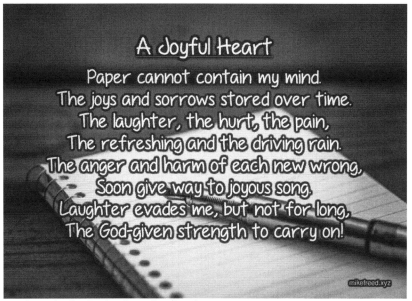

Created with a Pixabay Image from Pexels

Chapter Seven

Ruminations and Regurgitations of a Bipolar Mind

"Since, then, you have been raised with Christ, set your hearts on things above, where Christ is, seated at the right hand of God. Set your minds on things above, not on earthly things. For you died, and your life is now hidden with Christ in God. When Christ, who is your life, appears, then you also will appear with him in glory." (Colossians 3:1-4 NIV)

As I mentioned in chapter one of this book, I battle a condition called bipolar affective disorder. In the pages that follow you will find expressions of the highs, lows, and angry mixed states, common in this illness. In addition, you will find my attempts to make sense of it all and manage its many facets.

Some days the battle is easy, and I am lulled into thinking that I have conquered the beast. Inevitably though, sometimes in small ways and sometimes in big, it rears its ugly head. How I long for the day when God will wipe away every tear and remove every vestige of not only my illness, but of all sin, sickness, and death.

Depression

Depression sits like a frightened rabbit,
So paralyzed by fear that he cannot move.

Depression envelopes like thick smog.
Like the acrid smoke of a battlefield,
It smells of death and tries to choke the life out of the survivors.

Depression waits patiently like a vulture, for its victim to die,
Depression wraps itself around you like an anaconda,
And squeezes the life out of you.
Depression feels like quicksand,
No matter how hard or how little you struggle,
You still, continue to sink.

Depression is close kin to death, slow, slow suicide.

> **I am overwhelmed with troubles and my life draws near to death. I am counted among those who go down to the pit; I am like one without strength. I am set apart with the dead, like the slain who lie in the grave, whom you remember no more, who are cut off from your care. You have put me in the lowest pit, in the darkest depths. (Psalms 88:3-6 NIV)**

I sincerely hope that you cannot relate to either the poem or passage above, because most likely that means that you have not experienced clinical depression. If you can relate, then try and take at least some small comfort in the fact that you are not alone! In fact, statistics suggest that between 10 and 25% of people will experience major depression in their lifetime. No pain is as real as your own and when you are in the middle of a major depression you may think that it will never end. You may feel that no one could experience the pain, loneliness, worthlessness, anger, grief, and/or utter despair that you are experiencing and live. **Suicide may seem the only option, it is not! Get help! Call the national suicide prevention lifeline at 1-**

800-273-8255 or one of the other local and national hotlines that are available by searching for them online. Make an appointment with a counselor! Visit the ER and get evaluated! Call 911 but get help! Depression almost always lifts, life is worth living, hang in there and get help!

I am not a professional, only a depression survivor, what follows is my list of tips that I have found helpful in managing my depression and mental health. A word of caution, don't try and do everything on the list at once, build gradually. Start with finding your professionals, especially a good counselor (my opinion), and build from there gradually implementing their suggestions and together formulating a plan of action which may include adding things from the list that seem easiest or most helpful.

1. Seek professional help! A doctor may be able to help you evaluate the situation and dispense medication if needed. **In my experience medication alone is seldom the solution and medications are not without side effects**, and some of them can be severe. **Often depression is triggered by the stresses and traumas of life, and a good counselor such as a psychologist or social worker can help you sort through them and develop strategies to deal with them and heal from them. One technique known as EMDR can be very effective, especially in dealing with trauma. Often the best results come from a mixture of modern medications and counseling techniques.** This is the route after much trial and error that I have chosen. Due largely to an ongoing relationship with an excellent counselor, I have since been able to come off my antidepressant medication, though I still take medication for other aspects of my bipolar condition.

2. Take responsibility for yourself and your treatment. The first step may be selecting the professionals that are a good fit for

you, not always easy to do, and depending on your situation you may have more or less choice in this. Look for options. Even within the "system" there may be choices if you ask. Be open and honest with your professionals, they can't help if they don't know what's going on. Be open to the suggestions and insights your professionals offer, especially if they are hard to hear. Often, we are most resistant and most blind to the things we most need to hear. So, listen to your professionals! Don't just assume, however, that they have all the answers. Read and research on your own. Discuss with your professionals how things are going. Ask questions! Ask for "homework!" Do your best to put their suggestions into practice. Remember the more work you put in, the more you will likely get out. All this is easier said than done when you are in the midst of a major depression, so just do your best. Be patient with yourself and your professionals, and if after a reasonable time you are not improving it may be, I stress may be time, to seek out other help.

3. Manage sleep - Proper sleep is one of the most important things for mental health and health and wellbeing in general. Usually managing sleep means getting enough good and restful sleep. Sometimes with depression, however there can be a tendency to over-sleep which can perpetuate depression. You may wish to monitor your sleep habits and discuss them with your professionals.

4. Get out and around people. Do things with friends or find a support group. When stressed and depressed often our reaction is to isolate. Science and countless cases of experience tell us this is the wrong thing to do. So, use some of your limited willpower to get out and around people.

5. Think realistically, even positively. Negative, catastrophic, absolute thinking patterns perpetuate depression. Try and catch them and practice rephrasing them to more realistic and positive statements. (For example: Instead of I am always depressed, and it will never end. Try, I am going through a difficult time right now, and I will get better.) A good counselor can help you with this. You may even want to count or make a list of the good things in your life. Cultivate that "attitude of gratitude." It is not easy, when you are depressed, but it can be done. Start small, writing down one or two things a day you are grateful for might be a start. Try and do it consistently every day. Small habits done consistently over time can multiply into big changes.

6. Exercise! It generates endorphins and other things that help us feel better. Start small, maybe even stupidly small, and try and do it often, every day if possible. Tell yourself I will do one push-up, or one jumping jack, or I will put my tennis shoes on and take one step out the door. If you do it, celebrate achieving your goal. You may want to even check it off on a calendar, so you can see how many times you have done it. If you feel like doing more once you have started, go for it. Sometimes, especially when you are depressed, getting started is the hardest part, so set very low expectations for success and watch them grow.

7. Love yourself! Let others love you! Let God love you! When you are depressed you often feel unlovable. You are not! You are just a person going through a tough time. Remember God loves you and wants the best for you! It is the devil who wants to keep you down and steal your joy!

> *"The thief comes only to steal and kill and destroy; I have come that they may have life, and have it to the full." (John 10:10 NIV)*
>
> *"Praise the Lord, my soul; all my inmost being, praise his holy name. Praise the Lord, my soul, and forget not all his benefits—who forgives all your sins and heals all your diseases, who redeems your life from the pit and crowns you with love and compassion, who satisfies your desires with good things so that your youth is renewed like the eagle's. The Lord works righteousness and justice for all the oppressed." (Psalm 103:1-6 NIV)*

As difficult as it might be, know that God loves you, and do your best to claim the above verses as your own!

8. Look for ways to love and serve others. Sometimes looking beyond ourselves can lead us to a better understanding and appreciation of ourselves.

9. Prayer, meditation, singing, uplifting music, relaxation techniques, journaling, art, making a collage, and other creative and spiritual activities may also prove helpful.

10. Be patient. All this takes time. Take small consistent steps as they seem helpful. Remember don't try and do everything on the list at once, build gradually.

<u>Some Days</u>

Some days I struggle! I must fight to stay sane!
I must fight to stay happy and to maintain a sense of joy and peace amidst the sorrow,
Amidst the evil and dark forces in the world!
I battle anxiety, fear, and depression!

I write to adjust my attitude,
To remind myself that I am a precious and dearly loved child of God!

I write to make my requests and feelings known to Him and to myself,
For, He already knows me better than I know myself.
I write to offer up my thanksgiving and praise to Him,
Though I suspect that this too is more for my benefit than His!
I write to regain my hope and my sense of purpose!

Some days I walk or exercise or swim,
Because these too seem to help in this battle.
Getting around people usually helps too,
Though sometimes I just need quiet solitude.
Some days are easier than others.
Some days are just hard!
Some days, I do pretty well!
Some days, I fail miserably,
And just give up...
Or give in for a while...

...but so far,
the will to go on, to try again,
has always, eventually returned!

Black Birds Wreaking Havoc (The Old Man Rails)

What things lurk in the subconscious mind?
Stored there, midst the eons of time.
Cain and Able, Esau too,
Bad, bad boy and little boy blue.
Some men paint, and some men fight,
Some men hide, and some men write.
Ramble, ramble, run, and run.
Run until the day is done.
Trying to escape the pain,
To wear it out or to gain...
Some new sense of happiness,

Wearing life amidst distress.

Life's a funny, funny game,
I'd laugh at it, were it not for Him.
My God looks over my shoulder and He frowns.
Nothing is good enough for Him I've found.
Is it Him or is it me?
One or the other it must be!
He is perfect, so it must be me!
And round and round I go.

I love Him, oh can't you see!
On a good day, I even love me!
But it's too much work and too much bother,
For I'm lazy and prone to death.

It doesn't rhyme, but neither does life,
Eve messed it up, blame Adam's wife!
Blame her, oh, blame her...
If someone must be blamed.
Throw her to the fire and flames!
Or blame Adam, or the snake,
Or blame God himself...
He made us after all!
It must be His fault!

I dance the fire; I tread hells door!
Thumb my nose at God; I've done that before!
I'm close, so close, to the brim...
Will my God push me in?

No, my God loves me - it's no trick!
He will not put out this smoldering wick!
No peace I find, so on I rhyme!
Vomiting, vomiting all the time!

*If I could just get all the garbage out of me,
I'd know the truth and it would set me free!*

*Sometimes poetry, sometimes prose,
Broken words and scrambled phrases.
I write, I write, just like I raced,
Clinging to God, but something out of place!
Complaining, complaining, always complaining...
So many words for which to account,
And their written down, not spoken out...
All the worse. Yes, all the worse!*

*I delight myself with delusions of grandeur!
Oh, you worm, don't you know,
You're eating holes in your very soul!
Don't you know it's a sin?
Blasphemy of the worst sort!
Don't you know that He wants to come in?
If only you would let Him!*

*Change the subject; take a different track!
You're good at that!
You know how to play all the angles,
But you still lose!
How about love -
Write about love -
What will you say?*

*Oh, love, yes, love, patient and kind,
Of the codependent kind,
It plays with my mind!
But I'm getting better each day,
Better, yes, better in the worst possible ways!*

I didn't change it. I'm in a rut!
Wake up and get your head out of your butt!
Garbage, garbage, nothing but garbage!
It must be - you wrote it!
Nothing good comes from Nazareth anyway!
An Israelite without any guile? -
"Expletive deleted", you're nothing but lies!
Listen, listen to the devil talk!
I write on I will not stop!
Like a child to a parent, I'll provoke my God!
Any response is better than none at all!

If I quit now, where will I run?
My mind rushes on,
On, on, on, on!
No! No! No! No! No!
Yes! Yes! Yes!
I'll be positive...
But no, yes, no, yes, creates such a mess!

How will I ever translate these hieroglyphics?
Peace, patience, happiness would sure be terrific!
Ramble and rage - maybe get paid?
A not-so-subtle pride lies within my hide!
And on and on I go ... Racking up the sins...

I cease to be honest,
This ceases to be helpful...
But will I quit?
I cannot!
I stuff myself with food!
I pommel myself with self-talk!
Addicted,
A moth to a flame,
I destroy myself and my loved ones with me!

Perhaps now I am beginning to make some sense.
If only I would listen!
But alas, I have neither "ears that hear" nor "eyes that see!"
I prefer darkness to light! Death to life!
Foolish man, oh, foolish pride, Turn to Him that you might not die.
Yes, Lord, forgive my sin!
And tomorrow we'll kill the old man, all over again!

NO! NO! NO! NO! NO!
Don't kill him!
Love him!
Forgive him!
Nurture and feed him!
Clothe him!
Hold him!
Heal him!
Redeem Him!
Recreate him!
For I am he!
And he is me!

... but if You must kill him, then resurrect him too,
To live a life in You!

> **Praise be to the God and Father of our Lord Jesus Christ! In his great mercy he has given us new birth into a living hope through the resurrection of Jesus Christ from the dead, and into an inheritance that can never perish, spoil or fade... (1 Peter 1:3-4 NIV)**

> **You were taught, with regard to your former way of life, to put off your old self, which is being corrupted by its deceitful desires; to be made new in the attitude of your minds; and to put on the new self, created to be like God in true righteousness and holiness.**
> **(Ephesians 4:22-24 NIV)**

Memories, Outlooks & Emotions

The birds came home to roost today,
The birds came home to nest.
Starlings, sparrows, blackbirds, and cardinals with the rest.
Yes, the birds come home, day by day,
But I only let the cardinals stay.

> **Finally, brothers and sisters, whatever is true, whatever is noble, whatever is right, whatever is pure, whatever is lovely, whatever is admirable—if anything is excellent or praiseworthy—think about such things. (Philippians 4:8 NIV)**

A Note From Dad

My precious child,
My precious child, do whatever your heart desires,
And do it well!
I am glorified by many things,
But depression and despair are not among my attributes.
When you hear the music start, then join in the dance!

> **You turned my wailing into dancing; you removed my sackcloth and clothed me with joy, that my heart may sing your praises and not be silent. Lord my God, I will praise you forever. (Psalm 30:11-12 NIV)**

A Psalm of Desperation and God's Response

In my sinfulness and depression, I called out to the Lord and He heard my prayer! I said, "I cannot endure this pain!" and He took it upon Himself! I cried out, "I am dying!" and He restored my life! The evil one would steal our joy! He would have us believe that God, our Father wants to hurt and harm us! But God has said, "Never will I hurt you, never will I desert you! I am with you always in good times and in bad! I will walk with you and carry you! I will wipe every tear from your eye! I will plant you as a tree beside a stream, as flowers of the field you shall flourish and reproduce! I will clothe you with garments of the finest linen and feed you with all good things! I will restore to you a thousand-fold what the evil one has taken from you! You will remember your former life no more!"

Bipolar Beatitude

Sing, Sing, Ring, Ring, Rhyme, Rhyme all the time,
Trying to make sense out of a mind that moves to quickly.
Out of words of despair, that won't be fenced.
Forgive me, Father, if I blaspheme,
But perhaps I cannot help it,
For I have met the demon and named him too,
And the demon, he is me!
It will not work to cast him out,
For he'll only return with his friends,
Then with a vengeance, they'll party hardy,
Until they become my end!
But beloved, You make all things new,
And the two shall be as one,
Reconciled in Christ, the wall broken down,
The wolf and the lamb become friends!

> **But now in Christ Jesus you who once were far off are made near in the blood of Christ. For he is our peace, who made both one, and broke down the middle wall of partition, having abolished in the flesh the hostility, the law of commandments contained in ordinances, that he might create in himself one new man of the two, making peace; and might reconcile them both in one body to God through the cross, having killed the hostility thereby. He came and preached peace to you who were far off and to those who were near. For through him we both have our access in one Spirit to the Father. (Ephesians 2:13-18 WEB)**

Progress at Last

Simple Surgery-
Age 3 – Deserted – Alone - Surgical Ward –

Operating table cold - Blanket wrapped tight - People speak -
All a buzz - Wearing green - Bright lights shining ...

Then the mask - It engulfs my face – Ether - Terrible caustic stuff -
I struggle and fight - Anxiety out of control - I curse and cry -
Trying to control the uncontrollable ...

Age 3 - Simple surgery - ***Trauma for life*** *- Deserted*
Alone - Anxiety out of control - I curse and cry -
Trying to control the uncontrollable

EMDR *-*
57 years later - Pulsers buzz -Comfortable chair-
Therapist speaks - Soothing words - Then quiet -Pulsers buzz -
Eyes close - Memories return –
The Mask - Big and Bold - Engulfing my face –
Deserted – Alone - Cursing and crying - Anxiety out of control -
Trying to control the uncontrollable

The Mask - Big and Bold - Engulfing my face -
Memory growing smaller now - Pulsers buzz -
It moves to the left - Smaller still - More distant -It fades –
Pulsers stop - Therapist speaks -Soothing words - Deep breath -
Eyes open - Life returns ...

Progress -
Still work to do…

Self-Talk

Oh, such words I say to myself,
"Worthless! Useless! Hopeless elf!"
I pommel myself with these and worse,
Yes, with words, I cannot repeat in verse!

Why do I not say?
"Created in God's image! Redeemed! Precious! Talented!
Loved and loving!"
In Jesus Name! Amen!

> **But you are a chosen people, a royal priesthood, a holy nation, God's special possession, that you may declare the praises of him who called you out of darkness into his wonderful light. (1 Peter 2:9 NIV)**

Melancholy and Madness

Dear God,
Some days you just need to sit with your melancholy or your madness.
To take it all in without judging it or trying to fix it.
Sometimes it's nice to have a friend to sit with you in quietness,
Or to embrace you in love,
Perhaps to listen to your rambling and raging,
Or to put on soothing music and remind you to be still.
I love you God.
Thanks for sitting with me and being there in my sorrow,
And in my joy.
For being there through the mundane, the majestic, and the madness.
You are a faithful father, savior, brother, and friend!

> **If I go up to the heavens, you are there; if I make my bed in the depths, you are there. If I rise on the wings of the dawn, if I settle on the far side of the sea, even there your hand will guide me, your right hand will hold me fast. (Psalm 139:8-10 NIV)**

Glorious Day, Long Lonely Night

Once, oh Lord, You lifted me to heights, I couldn't even imagine.
You opened heaven within heaven,
Revealed mysteries in a moment, held secret for ages!

Gave me words to utter, and words to conceal.
Made the assurance of knowing Christ,
Joyfully, painfully, magnificently real!
No one wants to talk much about that day.
Each one hopes that, somehow,
The other will explain it all away.
Charismata or mania?
The joy, the agony, the fear,
Sometimes makes me hesitant to draw near.
To read,
To write,
To risk the pain,
The ridicule, of the sane.
Let not the bitterness and despair overwhelm me,
Nor the glorious heights derail me.
Make thy way, my way, plain before me!

> *I know a man in Christ who fourteen years ago was caught up to the third heaven. Whether it was in the body or out of the body I do not know—God knows. And I know that this man—whether in the body or apart from the body I do not know, but God knows— was caught up to paradise and heard inexpressible things, things that no one is permitted to tell. I will boast about a man like that, but I will not boast about myself, except about my weaknesses.*
> *(2 Corinthians 12:2-5 NIV)*

> *When the members of the Sanhedrin heard this, they were furious and gnashed their teeth at him. But Stephen, full of the Holy Spirit, looked up to heaven and saw the glory of God, and Jesus standing at the right hand of God. "Look," he said, "I see heaven open and the Son of Man standing at the right hand of God." At this they covered their ears and, yelling at the top of their voices, they all rushed at him, dragged him out of the city and began to stone him. Meanwhile, the witnesses laid their coats at the feet of a young man named Saul. (Acts 7:54 -58 NIV)*

> *He has shown you, O mortal, what is good. And what does the LORD require of you? To act justly and to love mercy and to walk humbly with your God. (Micah 6:8 NIV)*

A Joyful Heart

Paper cannot contain my mind.
The joys and sorrows stored over time.
The laughter, the hurt, the pain,
The refreshing and the driving rain.
The anger and harm of each new wrong,
Soon give way to joyous song.
Laughter evades me, but not for long,
The God-given strength to carry on!

> **When the Lord restored the fortunes of Zion, we were like those who dreamed. Our mouths were filled with laughter, our tongues with songs of joy. Then it was said among the nations, "The Lord has done great things for them." The Lord has done great things for us, and we are filled with joy. (Psalm 126:1-3 NIV)**

> **…. Shout for joy to the LORD, all the earth. Worship the LORD with gladness; come before him with joyful songs. Know that the LORD is God. It is he who made us, and we are his; we are his people, the sheep of his pasture. Enter his gates with thanksgiving and his courts with praise; give thanks to him and praise his name. For the LORD is good and his love endures forever; his faithfulness continues through all generations. (Psalm: 100 NIV)**

The Philosopher's Unexpected Surprise

How many angels can dance on the point of a pin?
Six-Sixty-Six, and we're dancing with them.
Deceitful discernment, we whirl end to end,
Oblivious to the obvious oblation of sin.
Good equals bad; bad equals good,
Life, long, has ceased to rhyme as it should.
Then, whoosh, without warning, the Christ enters in!
Destroying the demons and our pointed pretend!
Yanked from our superfluous, sick, sinful spin,
Joy of joys, we're now dancing with Him!

> *Praise the Lord. Sing to the Lord a new song, his praise in the assembly of his faithful people. Let Israel rejoice in their Maker; let the people of Zion be glad in their King. Let them praise his name with dancing and make music to him with timbrel and harp. For the Lord takes delight in his people; he crowns the humble with victory. (Psalm 149:1-4 NIV)*

Freedom at Last

Oh, Father, I know how the devils can dance,
The havoc they can wreak!
I know how they can infect the mind,
Placing body and soul in jeopardy.
In my weakness and willfulness, they overcome me
And sin has its day!
Sin may reign for a day; its effects may linger for a lifetime,
But Your love endures forever!
In Your strength, I will take refuge!
In Your love, I will dwell safely!
In the shadow of Your cross; in the coolness of Your empty tomb,
I will find forgiveness, freedom, and healing!

> *The thief comes only to steal and kill and destroy; I have come that they may have life, and have it to the full. (John 10:10 NIV)*

To ponder, journal and/or perhaps share:

1. Medieval philosophers and theologians supposedly argued about such things as how many angels could dance on the head of a pin or the point of a needle, what things do you argue about that probably aren't that important? (It may help to remember a specific incident.)

2. Of the poems in this chapter, which one do you most relate too? Why?

3. Of the scriptures in this chapter, which one gives you the most comfort or encouragement?

4. What is the most depressed you have ever been? What helped you get out of it?

5. What are some of the "traumas" you have experienced that still affect you today?

6. Has there ever been a time when you felt a special closeness to God? If so when was it?

7. How honest are you with yourself and with God? Have you ever been angry with God? Blamed God? Cursed God?

8. What has "the thief" tried to steal, kill or destroy in your life?

9. What if anything, is your "God-given strength to carry on?"

10. Has anything ever caused you to be hesitant about drawing near to God? What, if anything?

11. What words do you speak to yourself that you would like to change?

12. What "music" do you hear in your life? What "dance" is God calling you to join in?

Painted by Karlie with Assistance from Paint the Town -Wichita

Painted by Karlie with Assistance from Paint the Town -Wichita

Painted by Karlie with Assistance from Paint the Town -Wichita

Chapter Eight

Pray, Praise, Give Thanks or Complain, but be Honest with God

"This, then, is how you should pray:
"'Our Father in heaven, hallowed be your name, your kingdom come, your will be done, on earth as it is in heaven. Give us today our daily bread. And forgive us our debts, as we also have forgiven our debtors. And lead us not into temptation, but deliver us from the evil one.'" (Matthew 6:9-13 NIV)

Rejoice in the Lord always. I will say it again: Rejoice! Let your gentleness be evident to all. The Lord is near. Do not be anxious about anything, but in every situation, by prayer and petition, with thanksgiving, present your requests to God. (Philippians 4:4-6 NIV)

The Prayer of my Youth

It's foolish, Father, to think that we can be something that we're not. I could put up a front and pretend that I believe everything I've traditionally been taught and push down the questions and the doubts, but how would I ever grow.

So, I let it all hang out, the good and the bad. I read Your word and I trust that You will reveal Yourself to me - that You will lead me to true faith! That You will teach me all I need to know.

Father, I'm in Your hands - be gentle!

I frequently begin my day by "journaling." Most often my journal entries take the form of prayers that start "Dear Dad," then I simply write whatever comes into my head. Sometimes profound, often mundane, and occasionally profane, I simply pour out whatever comes to mind, "the good, the bad and the ugly" as they say. When I began this process, there was indeed plenty of "bad and ugly" and I was quite a complainer. In the last several years however, I have increasingly discovered the power of praise and thanksgiving. So now, even if I start in a negative vein, I usually catch myself and transition quickly to thanking and praising God. When I do this, my spirit and mood are often uplifted, and I come away with a more positive attitude about things. It's not a perfect formula, but it seems to help.

Within these prayers I noticed that some of my words echoed the sentiments, language, and style of the Psalms. The psalms are among the most read and most beloved of all the books of the Bible. Originally meant to be sung, they were in many respects the Jewish songbook. While praise and thanksgiving are certainly prevalent in the Psalms you will also find loud laments of desperation and depression, cries for forgiveness and words of prophecy, proclamation, and instruction. These (as well as some good old fashion complaining) are reflected in my prayers and psalm-like writings recorded here.

I have endeavored to include a balanced selection, but I have edited out some of the more "everyday petitions." Our God, who numbers even the hairs on our head, is certainly concerned with the daily details and dramas of our lives and we should certainly bring them to Him. I was not so sure that my readers would be as interested in prayers for my family and friends, complaints about conflicts with coworkers, or laments about blown head gaskets, failing water heaters, or backed-up sewers.

So why do I begin my prayers "Dear Dad," instead of with something more formal and reverent such as "Dear Heavenly Father" or

"Most Gracious Heavenly Father"? The simplest answer is that is how I most often addressed my earthly father; for me it is a term of affection, relationship, and respect. I believe that God would like us to come to Him as we would our earthly father, to come as little children. It is a tremendous privilege He has given us as His children, and I am cognizant that this privilege was bought for us at a high price. Though I am often awed by this privilege, I see nothing wrong with addressing our Heavenly Father as dad or even daddy. I mean no disrespect by it. Your family might be different but around our house Father was used only in referring to someone in the third person, never as a direct address. It was always dad or daddy. If my use of Dad or Daddy poses a stumbling block to you, simply insert whatever address feels comfortable.

Dear Dad, You are an awesome God! Thank You for this day! Help me to live it in gratitude and service to You and in love of all people!
In Jesus Name, Amen!

Praise God, all you people! Write and sing songs of praise! Praise Him from the lowest to the highest among you!

He brings good things out of evil! The evil one intended our destruction, but God, our God, the great Father of all, has redeemed us and brought about our deliverance and salvation! Sing praise all you people! Call upon His Name! His name is Yahweh, the great I AM! His name is Jesus, God-saves! His name is Love! Call upon our God! Dwell in His presence; open your hearts to His Spirit! Live and move and have your being in Him! Joyous and Wonderful is His name! Counselor and Mighty God! God of God and Light of Light!

Who can fathom His being or label His great goodness? Though we build bigger and better boxes, they cannot contain Him! He confounds the wise and reveals Himself to the lowly!

Great is our God and greatly to be praised! In the city and upon the mountain, sing praise! As you rise up and as you lie down, praise our God! At noontime and as you head to and from work, sing of His mighty deeds and His great love for us! Morning, noon, and night, praise Him without ceasing! In good times and bad, in easy times and hard, give Him unceasing thanks and praise!

He stoops down to lift you up! He forgives all your sins! He runs to meet you with outstretched arms! Sing praise and thank Him!

<u>A Double Prayer for no Particular Reason</u>

Dear Dad, I love You, but not sure my whole heart is in it right now. Be with me this day and week. It's shaping up to be busy. Draw me close to You! Keep me ever mindful of Your love! Teach us to love and trust You and others as we did when we were children. Restore our faith and our love which You have so generously poured out on us.
In Jesus Name, Amen!

Dear Dad, what a privilege to call you Dad! You are the God and Father whose love endures forever! Your mercy and your justice cause the children of men to glorify your name! God of God and light of light! Creator, source and person, spirit, and being!

We cannot fathom your existence; our minds boggle when we try to put all the pieces together, but we believe you made us! We believe you love us! We believe you have our best interest at heart! We believe that your essence is love and goodness, justice, and mercy!

You weave a web of events that work out for the good of your children! You make all things new in you! You bring us back into a relationship of oneness with you! Thy kingdom come! Thy will be done! Good Spirit of life and truth, dwell in us, and surround us! Let us live and move and have our being in You! Let us abide in You and bear much fruit!

Light of Light and very God of very God transform us into beings of Your light and love! Transform us into living vessels that pour Your love and life into others! Become a spring of life and love welling up from within us and overflowing with love and goodness, justice, and mercy! Thy kingdom come! Thy will be done!

Bring us light and love to see us through every easy and difficult situation! Let our trust be in you! Let our hope and our joy and our peace be in you! Give us wise, loving forgiving and generous hearts and minds! Thy kingdom come! Thy will be done!

Infinite wisdom from above, keep us this day and always! Protect us from evil! And keep us from sin and temptation! Let us not be wise in our own eyes but fill us with humility and mercy! Let us walk humbly with you! Let us walk courageously with you! Let us act justly and love mercy! Thy kingdom come! Thy will be done!

Amen and Amen! In Jesus Name Amen! You are goodness and light! Your love endures forever! Amen!

Praise our great God! Praise our Daddy, God! Loving and caring! Strong and Mighty! He loves us with an everlasting love!

Love the Lord, all you people! Sing, dance, and give praise to our God! He could crush us like bugs, but instead He makes us His children!

What a God! No other being is like Him! Sing Praise!

Dear Dad, who is like You, mighty in power, but loving, companionate, and forgiving! You do not hold our sins against us, but forgive! Hear us, Father, and forgive us! Though our sins are many, restore us to Yourself! Put an end to hatred and violence.! Open our hearts, to love and to serve!

I pray also for my enemies, those who would do me harm! Turn their hearts toward You! And I pray, as strange as it may sound, for Satan and all his angels! If it is possible turn them from their evil ways to love and follow You! And I pray for myself, because sometimes I am my own worst enemy! Teach me to forgive, those around me, the devil, and his demons for their evil actions and myself for all my shortcomings and sins! Hear us for Your namesake and the sake of Your Son! In Jesus Name, Amen!

For our struggle is not against flesh and blood, but against the rulers, against the authorities, against the powers of this dark world and against the spiritual forces of evil in the heavenly realms. (Ephesians 6:12 NIV)

Your mercies are new every morning! Your loving kindness rises with the dawn; at midday, You refresh us, and in the evening You close our eyes in peace!

How can we ever repay You for all Your tender mercies, for Your acts of kindness both great and small! I said, "I will confess my sins unto the Lord!" and You forgave all my unrighteousness!

Come to Him, all you who are heavy laden, and you will find rest for your souls! Come to Him, you who are weary from long days of burden, for He will give you rest and peace! He pardons all our sins! He clothes us in His righteousness! He takes off our filthy rags, washes us, binds up our wounds, and wraps us in clean linen!

Our God is a great God and greatly to be praised! From the rising of the sun to its setting, He brings light and life to our existence! He stoops down to bare our shame and raises us up into glory with Him!

Turn around, dear friend! Repent of your evil ways and trust our God and Father! He wants nothing more than to love and care for you! His anger lasts for a moment; His loving kindness to all generations! The Lord forgives those who come to Him! He seeks them out and bears them up on His shoulder as a shepherd carries a lamb he loves, as a daddy carries a precious child!

Dear Dad, teach us Your ways, oh Lord! Teach us Your ways! Let my eyes see and behold! Let them gasp with amazement at Your goodness and mercy! Teach us Your ways, oh Lord.! Make us kind and loving, generous, merciful, and gracious!

Hear our cry, oh Lord! Father God listen to our plea! Ten times... no one thousand times ten thousand times we have turned away from You, but You welcome us back! Teach us; lead us; save us or we perish!

In Jesus Name, Amen!

In my sin, I said, "Depart from me!" for who can stand in Your presence? None can stand, except those whom the Son has redeemed; those whom the Holy One has clothed with His righteousness!

Therefore, I will stand in the judgment and proclaim the goodness and forgiveness of the Righteous One! Therefore, I will speak on my brother's behalf, for I am like him! My God forgives and forgets! He remembers our sin no more! For the sake of His Son, He pardons every one of us!

Therefore, proclaim His goodness to your neighbor, His loving kindness to a generation yet unborn! Great is the Lord and greatly to be praised! He dares to be called our Father! He adopts us as His chosen children!

Praise the Lord, oh, my soul!

Dear Dad, bad day yesterday and really a bad week! Only You and I know how bad it was.

Oh Father, whose mercies are new every morning, forgive my sin and restore to me the joy of my salvation. Fill me with Your good Spirit that I may walk in Your ways and love You with all my heart, soul, mind, and strength. Protect me from pride but give me courage to live my life well and do what You would have me to do! Grant wisdom to guide me along the way, and love to sustain myself and others.

I get so scared and I put off doing things, then when I try something goes wrong and I am defeated. Lift me up, oh God! Set me on my feet again! Sustain me as crutches and braces! Give new life to my body and soul and set me once again on a right path! Make thy way plain! Give me a plan and a purpose and a mission.

In Jesus Name, Amen!

Wild-Eyed Imaginings - I think God Told Me to Put This Here (but maybe not)

Father make us one in you! Make us light and life and love! Make us Your beloved children; make us vessels of light and laughter and love!

Let us walk humbly and courageously with you all the days of this earthly life, then receive us into your glory and oneness to be born again in newness of life and hope, to be resurrected into the life and love that does not die!

I ramble and write of that which I do not know! Oh, how we long to know you and to know that you know us and love us! Forgive us and renew us good Father!

Fount and source and sustainer of light and life and love, dwell in us and around us! Go before us and be our rear guard! Light of Light and Love of Love, give our lives plan and purpose and hope!

In our pride and in our desire to please you and serve others, we propose to do great things! But you, oh God, are a God that multiplies the small and insignificant things, the humble things! You make the common, miraculous! You perform miracles with fish and bread, water and wine, mud and spit, and bodies of flesh and blood!

Whether we do seemingly insignificant things or great in this world is of little consequence. What counts are the miraculous works You do in us and through us! Works we are not always privileged to see. You take our ideas and actions and prayers; you bless them and multiply them and carry them out in your perfect timing; sometimes immediate-

ly and sometimes a thousand generations later! I am the beneficiary of the works and prayers of generations of people from Adam and Eve until the present, people of renown and people of obscurity! Most especially, I am the beneficiary of the works and prayers of Jesus of Nazareth, the Christ, my savior and master, mentor, brother, and friend!

Therefore, I lift my voice and pen my words for children yet unborn, for seemingly lost souls, for the evil and the good, for the dying and the despairing, saying, "Lord have mercy!" Crying out, "Father save us!"

I cry out for those yet unborn and those long dead, saying, "Let us find hope in You and in Your Son! I cry out for a world, not yet fully seen or known, where God dwells in our midst! Where all love and care and nurture each other! Where all give thanks and praise to the One, that is You!

Oh, Father God, I'm slipping into words I do not know the meaning of, words of prophecy, perhaps, and of hope, and desire, and longing! Words that I dare only to dream! But You, oh God are the God who does more than we dare to dream, or hope, or can even imagine! You are the God who brings into being, joy and goodness and peace, beyond belief!

Therefore, I will offer up my crazy imaginings! Therefore, I will cry, "Bring all souls to repentance and forgive them, as you have forgiven me!" Even now, I see it in my mind's eye! Around the world, hearts being opened to you! Opened to who you truly are and opened to love others as their selves!

Come, Lord Jesus, Come! Come blessed Spirit, come! Come and transform the lives of your people!

Let my prayers find the ear of my God! Let him roar with laughter and proclaim, "Is that all you can imagine, a world in which all are transformed and forgiven and saved? You ain't seen nothing yet!"

God who laughs at lightyears; God, who creates world upon world, universe upon universe; ever-expanding Source of oneness and being, who deigns to live within us and surround us; transform us with

Your presence and make us children of light! Bless us now, with the immeasurable, ever-expanding light of your love and help us to walk humbly and courageously with you!

Truly you are a God who does immeasurably more than we can think or ask or imagine! Accept our humble prayers and our wild-eyed imaginings! Let them find their "Yes!" in You and in Your Son! In His name we are bold to pray! His name we are bold to proclaim, saying, "YAHWEH saves! Blessed be the name of YAHWEH!" Amen! and Amen! In Jesus Name, Amen!

> **Now to him who is able to do immeasurably more than all we ask or imagine, according to his power that is at work within us, to him be glory in the church and in Christ Jesus throughout all generations, forever and ever! Amen. (Ephesians 3:20-21 NIV)**

Dear Dad, God of God and light of light! Who are you and from where do you come? From everlasting to everlasting, you are God! Yahweh we name you! Father Son and Spirit, we comprehend you! But you are beyond comprehension, beyond searching out! We cannot fully comprehend or know you. Your works and your ways are beyond us! Yet we know you are good! We know you are God! In you we live and move and have our being. When we sit and ponder your being, we are carried away to places it is probably not wise for us to go! Let us be still and know that you are God. Let us humble ourselves and walk humbly and courageously with you! Love us, lead us and make us your own! Amen and Amen in Jesus Name Amen!

Breathe in; breathe out; give thanks! For you have no life of your own, only that which the Holy Wind ordains and sustains! Write, oh man, and give thanks, for the words you write are not your own, they are a gift to you and to the world! Sow seed, oh farmer, and give thanks, for the Lord will produce a harvest in due time! Laugh, oh little one, and give thanks, for joy comes in the morning, a Christmas gift from your loving Father and dear Brother! Breathe in; breathe out; give thanks!

Dear Dad, You know the secrets of my heart; the hidden thoughts and actions I tell no one else; the masks I put on; the things I hide! Purify me, that I may not putrefy in my sin! Clean out every thought and desire that does not come from You! Even as I confess, I know that I will fall again! My heart is not pure! Purify me, oh Spirit of life!

I'm hedging on things. There are things I'm not quite ready to give up. Work in my life! Grow in me Your fruit; love, joy, peace, patience, kindness, goodness, gentleness, faithfulness, and self-control, and a pure heart that I may not sin against You or others! In Jesus Name, Amen!

Out of the depths of anguish and despair, I cry to You, good Father! Lift me out of this pit!

I tremble and am afraid; yet, there is no enemy that I can see! Fear and anxiety consume me, and when I say I will be brave, that I will take courage and accomplish something, my energy is anger! What little I accomplish, I do so with cursing and violence and end in crying over all I have said and done!

Good Father, You bid me to be courageous and to fear nothing for You are with me! Yet, tears fill my eye, all day long and I hide from them in what sleep I can find! What are these demons that plague me? Demons of anxiety, panic, depression, and procrastination! I cannot seem to escape them! They live in me! I have fought them, and I have embraced them; fed them, and prayed for them, but they are never satisfied for long! They are a part of me! Long ago they protected me, but now they would destroy me!

Hear me, good Father! Restore my sanity and hope! Be thou my hope and life!

... Now is your time of grief, but I will see you again and you will rejoice, and no one will take away your joy. In that day you will no

longer ask me anything. Very truly I tell you, my Father will give you whatever you ask in my name. Until now you have not asked for anything in my name. Ask and you will receive, and your joy will be complete. (John 16:22-24 NIV)

Dear Dad, Abba, Father, I do love You but I have not been showing it much lately and I have not loved myself or others as I should! I have strayed into overeating, willful eating, procrastination, and more! Forgive my sin! Forgive me and restore me!

In Jesus Name, Amen!

I will praise the Lord for all His marvelous deeds! But let not my words ring hollow! No, let my actions reflect the glories of our God! Let love and compassion be in all I do! Let justice and mercy rule my life! For what does God want from us, but to act justly, love mercy, and walk humbly with Him!

Praise God in all you do! Let your actions reflect the greatness of our God! Let your actions reflect His goodness and mercy that all people may glorify our God, that they may turn to Him and be saved! Praise be to God!

Dear Dad, I'm so filled with anxiety this week. I can't seem to center myself for long and when I do, I still don't get done some of the things I need too.

I love You, Father! I know You love me but, sometimes, it's hard to feel it or believe it. Abba, Father, take me in Your arms and hold me! Wrap me in Your love! Forgive me all my sins and shortcomings! Restore to me the joy of Your salvation, Your saving grace in Your Son!

In You is light and life! In You is joy and security! Keep me, good Father! In You is "gladness amidst all sadness!"

In Jesus Name, Amen!

There is joy in Zion! Laughter and singing throughout the world! Rejoice, oh Jerusalem, shout and sing all you peoples, for our God comes to save you and secure your hope!

He comes with pardon in His arms and healing in His wings! He forgives all our shortcomings and sins! He binds up every broken limb and heals all our diseases!

Therefore, give thanks and sing praises!

Dear Dad, oh what joy You have put in my heart and yet my soul laments for those whose lives are so joyless, for those who don't know You, for those who are afflicted in so many ways; the hungry, the lonely, the mentally ill, the poor and even the "evil!"

If Your hand had not touched my life, if You had not turned me around, I would be as they are, without hope and without joy! I do not deserve such blessings! Yet, You fill my life with good things! Hear me for Your namesake! Hear me on behalf of all the lonely, the hurting, the dying, the unrighteous, the fearful!

Turn our hearts to You! Break them if You must, but do not crush us! For we have no hope but in You!

In Jesus Name, Amen!

I said, "I will confess my iniquity to the Lord," and He has forgiven my sin!

Seventy times seven and more, I have fallen and failed Him, and yet He loves and restores me! He clothes me in His righteousness and removes from me the filthy rags of my transgressions!

Therefore, I will praise Him and tell His great mercies to the nations!

Dear Dad, I love You and I am so grateful for all Your rich blessings. I can't even imagine the glories You have in store for us. This life even in a sin-riddled world is so marvelous! What must life with You in eternity be like?

But this life isn't so great for some! I think of the poor and disabled kids Linda works with! We went to their prom! There were kids in wheelchairs! I wanted to touch them and proclaim, "In the name of Jesus of Nazareth, rise up and walk!" Why didn't I? Why couldn't I? Someday, I think they will lead the parade into heaven, leaping and dancing and praising God!

I don't know what You have in mind for me, Father. In many ways I have had my rewards here on earth, so I would be privileged to just be a servant in Your household. "Thy kingdom come, thy will be done on earth as it is in heaven! " I love You, kind Father! Thank You for loving me; for sending Jesus to show and be the way to You! Be with me this day and help me to share Your love!

In Jesus Name, Amen!

More trustworthy is the grace of God, than all the best works of people! He gives generously to all out of His love!

Though trouble and hardship may come upon us through no fault of our own, or by our stupid actions, yet God is faithful and just, gracious and compassionate! He will not leave us in our distress and sin forever but will rescue us from every evil and malady! In the end, we will see God face to face and tremble, but a smile will break across His face and we will rejoice in the grace of our God and in His Son, the Christ, our Savior!

So. trust in the Lord no matter what befalls you! Trust in the great I AM! Rejoice in the Christ, the Savior of the world, and live in the Spirit that dwells within you!

I say do good and not evil! Act justly and love mercy! For who knows what a simple act of kindness may bring; what joy it may create in the heart of the giver or receiver; what life-giving change! So, love and give and be merciful, for you will make glad the hearts of many and save your very soul, though it is not your doing, but a precious gift from God!

Dear Dad, Abba, Father, You know us and want what's best for us! You work behind the scenes so, that if possible, all might be saved! Teach us to trust in You, knowing that You work all things out for our good!

We love You, kind Father, and are so grateful that You love us! Give us light to see the path for today and faith to trust that You will lead us safely home!
                In Jesus Name, Amen!

How great is our God! Early in the morning, I will sing Your praises; before the dawn etches the sky, I will shout for joy to my God! For You are a great God, not counting our sin against us, but forgiving us each time we turn to You!

How great is our God! How wonderful! Magnificent in awe and power, yet tender and loving! You, oh God, are strong and You, oh God, are loving! Who is there like the Lord, "I Am" of our Fathers, who made heaven and earth!

Dear Dad, I'm feeling worn out and beaten down for no particular reason. I have things to do and don't feel like doing any of them, so I thought I would at least come and write to You.

Just when I think I am doing alright, the roof caves in and I find myself in the midst of depression. I don't like the feeling, but often I'm too afraid, and don't want to do anything to pull myself out of it. I'm thinking of the things I need and want to do and feeling overwhelmed. I'm not sure what else to say. I should ask for Your help, but it seems so much easier to wallow in self-pity.

I love You, God! Help me! Give me courage, wisdom, and direction! Hear us, oh, God! I am weak and in despair! Everything seems hopeless! Yet, I will call out to You! I will cry to the God of my salvation! You raise me up from the pit! You strengthen my arms and legs as for battle! You give me the resolve to go on! I am tired and unwilling! Yet, at Your word I will arise, and go in Your strength!

Return to me Your joy, oh God! Be thou, my joy, my strength, and my song!
In Jesus Name, Amen!

Sing praise to our God! Shout it from the mountains! Type it on your keyboard! Hum it in the pool but give God praise!

It is He who answers our prayers and brings good things from His hand! It is He who turns evil into good, bringing blessing out of disaster! Though the mountains tremble and the nations are in turmoil around us, yet I will sing of God's great mercies, the forgiveness won by His Son! Who is like the Lord, laying down His life for sinners; bringing us back and calling us His children!

Therefore, give God praise for He has forgiven us all our iniquity! Praise Him in the morning before you rise! Let the first words of your mouth be, "God is good!" and when you lie down at night let your heart cry out, "God is my salvation! Thanks be to God!"

Dear Dad, I woke up angry this morning. Angry at myself for the time I wasted this weekend, angry because I overate, angry because I've been depressed. Sometimes it seems I must get angry to take action, but I don't like it! I can't seem to balance things or find a rhythm I'm comfortable with. All my instincts say get moving! And You say, to be still and know that You are God, to come to You and rest! So, at least for a few minutes, let me rest in You.

I will sing Your praise! In the morning, I will come to You and sing praises to my God! Sing praises, all ye lands! Sing praises, for great is our God!

I'm having trouble getting going, trouble singing Your praises this morning! Go with me today and give me a voice to sing Your praises!

In Jesus Name, Amen!

Who is like the Lord, mighty in power, yet humble in heart? Who gathers the broken into His arms? Who brings low the mighty men until they see their need for God? Just and merciful is our God, full of compassion and love!

Oh, you proud, bow down before Him! You wicked, turn from your evil ways! You who are afraid and lonely, run into His arms! None is like the Lord, forgiving the sinners though they turn from Him a thousand times or more! He calls them to repentance and welcomes them back into His arms! When they see the folly of their ways, when they cry out in desperation, He hears and forgives and calls them, "My son!" "My daughter!" "My child!" Though they spend their whole life wasting their inheritance, yet He restores to them their fortunes and more!

Do not begrudge God His great mercies, you who follow Him and seek after Him! For who made you and placed such faith in your hearts? Was it not the Lord? And if it is by God's grace that you are who you are, then do not begrudge God when He shows grace and mercy to your sister or brother! God knows the plans He has for each of us and it is for mercy and forgiveness, and restoration that He calls us!

Therefore, I say, walk humbly with your God and give Him praise for His great mercy!

> **Then Jesus told them this parable: "Suppose one of you has a hundred sheep and loses one of them. Doesn't he leave the ninety-nine in the open country and go after the lost sheep until he finds it? And when he finds it, he joyfully puts it on his shoulders and goes home. Then he calls his friends and neighbors together and says, 'Rejoice with me; I have found my lost sheep.' I tell you that in the same way there will be more rejoicing in heaven over one sinner who repents**

than over ninety-nine righteous persons who do not need to repent.
(Luke 15:3-7 NIV)

Dear Dad, in my willfulness and wantonness, I sin against You! Yet, I love You and run back to You! Whom else can I turn to? Do not forsake me or I die! Do not turn Your face from me! Forgive me for Your namesake! Turn me again to follow You alone! Restore me as a gatekeeper or servant! I am not worthy to be called Your son! Yet, You received the prodigal son? Receive me also! How many times can I sin against You and You receive me back? I love You, Lord! I am lost and in despair! How can I come into Your presence?

Give me voice to sing of Your great mercies; to sing the praise of my God and Father! To sing of the great love of His Son! You know the secrets of my heart and the dark place of my life and yet You call me beloved!

In Jesus Name, Amen!

Oh, Father, I am overwhelmed by Your goodness and grace, Your never-ending love and kindness!

Though the world rages around us, in You we will find rest and peace! You are our shalom, our hello and good-bye, our peace! How can we help but sing Your praises and proclaim Your great goodness and glory! You forgive our sins! You restore our wealth and position as sons and daughters. even though we have wasted our inheritance!

I'm overwhelmed by Your love and the lengths You would go to win us back! I'm overwhelmed by the obedience and love of Your Son, our brother, Jesus Christ! Overwhelmed by His unwillingness to not fight back! Overwhelmed by His forgiveness! He could have enjoyed a luxurious life with You, but He gave it up for us!

We love You, Lord and Father! We love You, because You love us! We love You, Jesus!

Dear Dad, I love You and all people, but some are hard to love! Some drag me down! Lift me up by Your good Spirit, that I may minister to myself and others! Lead me in the paths that You would have me go! Lift me up, kind Spirit; show me Your way! Open the floodgates of Your grace and mercy! Provide for all our needs and desires!

You are the God who rescues! You are the God that provides! You are the God that changes the hearts and minds and lives of Your people! Work in our lives! Make us Your new creation! Teach us to love You! To love others! To love ourselves! For how can we truly love others if we do not care for ourselves?

In Jesus Name! Amen!

We praise You! We acknowledge You to be the Lord, God, Creator, and Redeemer of all people! Look with mercy upon us, for without You we are but dust of the ground! Teach us to walk humbly and courageously with You, to love and encourage one another!

We love You, Father! Our actions and our checkbooks do not always reflect that, but we love You! You desire good things for us, and You work even evil out for our good! We love You, great Yahweh; the "I am" that made and sustains us!

Walk with us this day! Guide our every thought and action! Good Father, lead, confront and comfort us! Let the evil one have no power over us, no dominion in our lives! Guard us from pride and envy, from unbelief and discouragement!

I love You, Lord! Thank You for loving me and sending Your Son! Restore to me the joy of my salvation and give me the courage to share it with others! In the name of the Father and of the Son and of the Holy Spirit! Amen and Amen!

> **You did not choose me, but I chose you and appointed you so that you might go and bear fruit—fruit that will last—and so that whatever you ask in my name the Father will give you. This is my command: Love each other. (John 15:16-17 NIV)**

To ponder, journal and/or perhaps share:

1. How honest are you with God? Why is that?

2. What is the first prayer, song, hymn or psalm you remember hearing or learning? Do you still use it today?

3. Do your prayers tend to be long and rambling or short and to the point?

4. The author begins these prayers "Dear Dad." what is your favorite way of addressing God in prayer? Why?

5. Do you tend to be more formal or familiar when praying? Why is that?

6. The author has chosen not to include some of his more "mundane" or "everyday" kinds of prayers, do you feel that was a wise decision? Why or why not?

7. There is an old saying to "count your blessings." Make a list of the things for which you can give God thanks and praise.

8. As the author mentions, in addition to thanks and praise the Psalms also often include cries of distress. What things do you need to cry out to God about? What are the areas of distress, anxiety, fear, sorrow, or sadness in your life?

9. Sometimes Psalms and prayers contain confessions of sin or shortcomings. What sins or shortcomings still plague you?

10. Philippians 4:4 says to "Rejoice in the Lord always!" Do you think that is even possible? Why or why not?

11. Look again at Luke 15:3-7 as well as the story of the parable of the lost son (Luke 15:11-32) Who do you relate most to in these passages, for example the lost sheep, the younger son or the older son? Why? What feelings do these passages evoke?

12. Which, if any, of these passages and prayers is your favorite? Why is that?

13. Which, if any, of these prayers or passages is your least favorite? Why is that?

14. Write your own prayer or psalm:

Created with a Pixabay Image from pixel2013

Created with a Pixabay Image from Alexas_Fotos

Chapter Nine

Table Scraps

A Canaanite woman from that vicinity came to him, crying out, "Lord, Son of David, have mercy on me! My daughter is demon-possessed and suffering terribly." Jesus did not answer a word. So his disciples came to him and urged him, "Send her away, for she keeps crying out after us." He answered, "I was sent only to the lost sheep of Israel." The woman came and knelt before him. "Lord, help me!" she said. He replied, "It is not right to take the children's bread and toss it to the dogs." "Yes it is, Lord," she said. "Even the dogs eat the crumbs that fall from their master's table." Then Jesus said to her, "Woman, you have great faith! Your request is granted." And her daughter was healed at that moment.
(Matthew 15:22-28 NIV)

Thanksgiving at our house included turkey! Unlike some, however, who carve the golden-brown bird at the table, we always "de-boned" it before bringing the meat to the table. After most of the meat was sliced and ready to serve there was the un-ceremonial "picking-of-the-bones" to remove the last bits of usable meat.

This job often fell to me, but I didn't mind because it was a legitimate way of sampling the bird before sitting down for the feast. The ritual went something like this, three or four scraps in the bowl, one for me and one for Jackie our rat terrier. All in all, quite a delicious and equitable arrangement, at least as far as Jackie and I were concerned. The tidbits collected in this chapter are short poems and phrases picked from the carcass of my journals after the main course had been carved away. Even so I think you will find many of them to your liking!

1

Taste and See

"Taste and see that the Lord is good,"
Like a pineapple cooled and sliced,
Like a watermelon cold, cubed, and cleared of seeds.

> **"The Lord is good to all; he has compassion on all he has made."**
> **(Psalm 145:9 NIV)**

2

Rebekah's Prayer
By Rebekah Freed -age 2

Thank You, God for Today!
Amen!

> ***God is our refuge and strength, an ever-present help in trouble. Therefore we will not fear, though the earth give way and the mountains fall into the heart of the sea, though its waters roar and foam and the mountains quake with their surging. There is a river whose streams make glad the city of God, the holy place where the Most High dwells. God is within her, she will not fall; God will help her at break of day (Psalm 46:1-5 NIV)***

3

To fall into the hands of an awesome God is a terrifying thing! To be received into the arms of a loving Father is joy upon joy!

4

In a Dry Land

One small flower clings to a half-dead plant,
The will to survive and thrive in a dry land,

Hope springs eternal,
A gift from the eternal hand!

#5

Water and blood and womb, and words,
"My beloved child!"
The breath of life,
A baptism and a birth,
Earthly parents,
A proud father, a faithful brother, and a kind spirit-mother!

#6

To love is a good thing, a God thing!
For God is love!
A noun, a verb, all parts of speech rolled into one!
My all in all, my source of being!
A good thing! A God thing!
I love You, God! Thanks for loving me!

#7

From the Mouths of Babes:
(by Elizabeth Freed as I remember them)

Mommy, "If Jesus took the punishment for all our sins, then how come you punished me when I ran out in the street?"

"Daddy, Jesus said we should pray for our enemies." "Yes, little one that's right." "Then does that mean we should pray for the devil?"

#8

"Waiting for the Lord I will let my heart take courage!" "I will wait, yes wait for the Lord!"

But now is the time to act!

Go up and seize the city, for the Lord is with you! Strong and mighty is His Name!
Wait no more, for your time is at hand!
Today is your salvation!
You have waited patiently, sometimes too patiently!
You have been double-minded and afraid to act, but your time has come!
Your God is with you! Your God goes before you!
The walls fall down! All the inhabitants plead for mercy!
Proclaim the salvation and deliverance of the Lord!
Teach them His ways and forgive all their sins!

9

I saw so many different birds this morning on my walk and as I sat on the front porch to drink my coffee; probably fifteen or twenty different species. I would see flashes of gray and brown and black in the trees and meadows, but also beige and white and red and orange and yellow and blue! How varied and majestic is Your creation and Your people!

10

If you think a pebble is insignificant, put it in your shoe and walk around on it for a day!

11

Writing is a narrowing and abridgment of the mind, but an expansion and focusing of the soul!

12

If you are not content where you are at, you probably won't be happy where you are going either!

13

All around there are people who have had terrible things happen to them, who live happy and productive lives!

14

<u>Morning Walk</u>

I took a walk on the farm this morning.
I heard a turkey gobble! I saw oriels and cardinals and a host of sparrows and birds I don't even know the names of!
I saw a red squirrel with a bushy tail! I saw wild asparagus growing! I picked up a couple of rocks, the jawbone of what I think was a 'possum, and a feather! What a wonderful way to start the day!
Spending time with You in Your wonderful creation!

15

I get so charged up each morning but often I fizzle out and fall short as the day goes on! Sustain my morning hope and trust! Turn it into God-pleasing action throughout the day!

16

Give all that you have to God, the seemingly rotten, with the ritually righteous, so that kings may feast, and dogs and pigs may be fed!

17

Accept my fish and bread, accept my life as a living sacrifice and bless it as only you can bless it! Provide an increase of 30, 50 100, 1000, 10,000, 100,000 or more, for you are the God of infinite blessing! You are the God who is not satisfied with the best returns of humans! You are the God who does miracles with the mundane! The God who gives Himself as mana! The God who exceeds our wildest hopes and dreams!

18

Repent for the kingdom of God is at hand! It will come in your lifetime, for either He will bring all things to an end or He will bring you to an end!

19

God's Kingdom is like a bottle of pop shaken until it bubbles over!

20

Sorrow and joy are both medicine for the soul!

21

Walk humbly with your God,
Do what is right,
Be merciful,
And sing praise!

22

Dearest Father,

Give our lives a plan and a purpose and draw us close to You!

23

Scripture is like medicine! But be careful that you do not take chemotherapy for a cold or aspirin for a cancer!

24

Sing praise to the Lord! Sing praise to our God!
Father and Son and Spirit are one!
Sing praise!

Sing Praise to the Father, our Daddy God!
Sing praise to the Son, our savior, brother and friend!
Sing praise to the Spirit, great counselor of hope!
Sing Praise!

25

The pain that God allows and the pain that God inflicts is not without love and purpose for us or our sisters and brothers!

26

Pheasant Faith

Flying Like a pheasant, I was shot down one glorious day,
But I hit the ground a-runnin' and lived to fly another day!

27

Loving people is messy business! Fortunately for us, God doesn't mind getting His hands dirty!

> **Who, being in very nature God, did not consider equality with God something to be used to his own advantage; rather, he made himself nothing by taking the very nature of a servant, being made in human likeness. (Philippians 2:5-7 NIV)**

28

Today's Reality, Tomorrows Hope

Nothing can separate us - You won't stop loving me!
So, Father, give me eyes that see,
It's so much more fun when I stop fighting You,
And join in the work we have to do!
And oh, there's so much more time to play,
When we take care of today's things, today!

29

The Puzzle Sits Completed

The puzzle sits completed,
Next to me on the table!
Put together with the help of friends,
The puzzle sits completed!
Except for one piece of missing sky,
And a small broken piece of flowers!
The puzzle sits completed!

30

In God's Time

Oh, most merciful God,
Words cannot contain my thoughts,
And medication cannot restrain Your joy!
Typing is to slow, but on I go.

#31

Never count out the mercies of God, for who can know what happens in that instant and eternity between life and death! Who can say if perhaps a loving father or a forgiving brother will not reach out to welcome a weary traveler home!

#32

Note to Self: Pursue your passions, but make sure they are in line with your principles!

#33

Father, show me the next step and give me the love, strength, and courage to take it!

#34

The best way to get motivated is to do something! Action breeds action!

#35

I think I heard this somewhere, but I've tried to make it my own: "The smallest act of kindness is greater than the biggest good intention!"

#36

Today I am content with what I have, who I am, and what I've done, because I'm Christ's!

37

I have noticed that sunsets are often more glorious than sunrises. Make the ending of our days, the beginning of even more glorious things, and help us to finish strong in You!

38

It is still dark outside, but Sunday has already come! We can barely glimpse the dawn of that bright new day, but He is risen! And one day, we shall need no sun or moon for He will be our light! The light of His love will shatter death and darkness and we shall shine like the stars! With the eyes of faith, we behold it! The light shines in the darkness! Hope is born anew! Shine children shine! He is risen indeed! Alleluia!

> *Do everything without grumbling or arguing, so that you may become blameless and pure, "children of God without fault in a warped and crooked generation." Then you will shine among them like stars in the sky as you hold firmly to the word of life...*
> *Philippians 2:14-16 NIV)*

> *The true light that gives light to everyone was coming into the world. He was in the world, and though the world was made through him, the world did not recognize him. He came to that which was his own, but his own did not receive him. Yet to all who did receive him, to those who believed in his name, he gave the right to become children of God— children born not of natural descent, nor of human decision or a husband's will, but born of God. (John 1: 9-13)*

> *I did not see a temple in the city, because the Lord God Almighty and the Lamb are its temple. The city does not need the sun or the moon to shine on it, for the glory of God gives it light, and the Lamb is its lamp. (Revelation 21:22-23 NIV)*

39

Love Us! Lead Us! Let the words "thy kingdom come, thy will be done" become the mantra and motivation by which we live!

#40

I suspect, that there may be many paths but only one way, even Jesus the Christ, who is the way the truth and the life!

> *Jesus answered, "I am the way and the truth and the life. No one comes to the Father except through me. If you really know me, you will know my Father as well. From now on, you do know him and have seen him." (John 14: 6-7)*

To ponder, journal and/or perhaps share:

1. What was your favorite food as a child?

2. What is your favorite food now?

3. What was Thanksgiving like at your house?

4. What is your first response to the way Jesus spoke to the Canaanite woman? What did you think of her reply?

5. How would your life change if you started each day with Rebekah's Prayer?

6. Is there one "scrap" you wish to hang on to and remember? If so which one and why?

7. Which is your least favorite "scrap"? Why?

8. What is one "scrap" of scripture that you know by heart?

9. If you could give someone some "table scraps" of your best wisdom, what would they be?

10. Are you content/happy where you are? Are there still places you would like to go? If so, what are some of those places?

11. What causes you to marvel at God's creation?

12. What is one area of your life in which you have waited patiently, but which God may be calling you to now take more deliberate and decisive action?

13. Recall a time you were "shot down" but lived to fly again.

14. What is one of the little perhaps seemingly insignificant things in your life that has a big positive or negative impact?

15. What are some of your life's passions? What are some of your highest principles? How well do they line up?

16. Who are some of the people who have helped to put together your life's puzzle? What are some of the pieces of that puzzle that are still broken or missing?

17. What is one area of your life in which you would like to finish strong? What is at least one thing you can do to help make that happen?

18. What do you imagine that "bright new day to be like?" How can we "glimpse" it in the here and now?

19. What is the mantra and motivation by which you are currently living? Are you satisfied with it? If not, how would you like to change it?

20. What is one of the most enjoyable "paths" you have walked in your life?

21. What is one of the most difficult "paths" you have walked in your life?

22. Who have been some of your favorite or most helpful traveling companions along the paths you've walked?

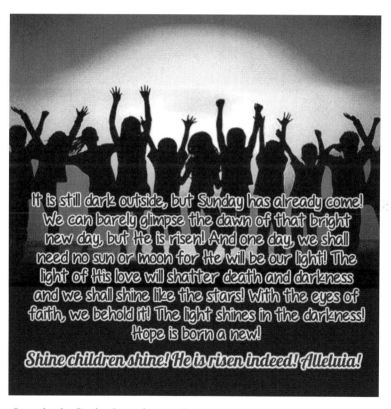

Created with a Pixabay Image from geralt

Created with a Pixabay Image from JanTemmel

Image Created by Karlie

Chapter Ten

Baskets Full of Leftovers!

When they had all had enough to eat, he said to his disciples, "Gather the pieces that are left over. Let nothing be wasted." So they gathered them and filled twelve baskets with the pieces of the five barley loaves left over by those who had eaten. After the people saw the sign Jesus performed, they began to say, "Surely this is the Prophet who is to come into the world." (John 6:12-14 NIV)

As I approached what I thought would be the end of this book, I noticed that one poem that I had planned to include was missing. On closer observation I noticed that another was missing, then another and another. When I finally found them in a back-up copy of the file I had been working on, I realized that there were even more pieces of writing than I had remembered, waiting to be woven into place. The task seemed overwhelming! I thought I was all but finished and now I had pages and pages I didn't know what to do with!

Then the story with which I began came back to mind. The story of the loaves and fish and the baskets, full of leftovers. That was what I had, proverbial basketfuls of leftovers! So, partly out of inspiration and partly out of desperation and laziness, I gathered them up into this chapter. In this hodgepodge of the forgotten poems and passages, I see a parable, if you will, of the kingdom of God.

Likewise, Christ's words, "Gather the pieces that are left over. Let nothing be wasted." resonate through my mind. I can't help but wonder if they are not filled with deeper, more prophetic, and profound meaning. I cannot help but wonder if this story too, does not contain a parable of the kingdom. It is my earnest hope and prayer that these broken and forgotten pieces of bread represent broken and forgotten people who will be gathered up lest anyone be wasted or lost.

In Search of my Sunday School Jesus

I woke up this morning thinking of a friend from High School, whom I haven't seen or spoken to in over 20 years. I said a quick prayer for her, as is my custom when people come to mind. Then I started lamenting the fact that I had never really shared Jesus with her. I wondered was I ashamed of this Jesus, my Jesus whom I love. And I wondered how I would feel if this friend, this friend, whom I probably wouldn't have made it through high school without, was not in heaven, because I had failed to speak with her and share with her, Jesus and His love and forgiveness. And she was not the only one!

I knew I needed to go and write, but I hesitated because I knew that writing couldn't fully convey all I was thinking and feeling and because I wasn't quite sure that I wanted to bare myself to the world. I knew that in the simple process of writing that my thoughts would be condensed and changed, that I would be changed. Yet after some hesitation and TV; here I am.

As I sit here my thoughts have changed and I'm left wondering, whatever happened to my "Sunday School Jesus?" It's hard to remember what I was like, or what I actually thought as a child, but I remember how my world changed the day someone told me that some people go to hell. Until that time, it was inconceivable to me that anyone would go to hell. You see in my "Sunday School World", God was Jesus and Jesus was God and everyone believed that. My "Sunday School Jesus" loved all people and had died so their sins were forgiven! When you died you went to heaven, not some people, but all people! In my "Sunday School World" people were basically good even if they sometimes did bad things. I loved everyone, and they loved me, even if we sometimes hurt each other.

Though it flies in the face of traditional Christianity, I still hold out hope for my "Sunday School Jesus" and my "Sunday School World".

> *He called a little child to him, and placed the child among them. And he said: "Truly I tell you, unless you change and become like little children, you will never enter the kingdom of heaven... "If anyone causes one of these little ones—those who believe in me—to stumble, it would be better for them to have a large millstone hung around their neck and to be drowned in the depths of the sea. Woe to the world because of the things that cause people to stumble! Such things must come, but woe to the person through whom they come! (Matthew 18:2-3; 6-7 NIV)*

> *On this mountain the Lord Almighty will prepare a feast of rich food for all peoples, a banquet of aged wine— the best of meats and the finest of wines. On this mountain he will destroy the shroud that enfolds all peoples, the sheet that covers all nations; he will swallow up death forever. The Sovereign Lord will wipe away the tears from all faces; he will remove his people's disgrace from all the earth. The Lord has spoken. (Isaiah 25: 6-9 NIV)*

This I Believe – Mike's Confession and Prayer

Dear Father, most Blessed Brother, Kind Spirit!

I have traveled the borderlands of theology, reason, heresy and beyond and You have traveled with me! You never left my side! I am perhaps no closer to a systematic theology or philosophy of life than when I began. I make no claims that I know my traveling companion any better than when I began, for how can one understand or contain the infinite in words, confessions, or creeds. Yet, I do believe!

This I believe, that You, oh God are strong and that You, oh God are loving! That You, oh God poured out Your life for us and that You oh, God give life and purpose!

This too, I believe that to love is a good thing, that to show mercy is God-like, that to forgive is healing to the soul! Yes, these things and many more I believe. I learned and relearned them on my journey, though most of them I already knew. Help my unbelief!

Oh, faithful companion, You never left my side! Sometimes You even carried me! Often, You pissed me off with Your words of truth and confrontation! Like knives through my soul, they cut deep to excise every evil! I cursed You and cussed You! I cried tears of loud laments in Your bosom! I ran from You and played the whore, but You never left me! You confronted and comforted me! I do not know whether, I have learned much on my journey, but this I have learned, to love my companion and to rest in His love and grace for me!

I love You, Dad! Are those just words I say, or do I demonstrate them in my actions and life? I do try, but sometimes I fail so miserably or perhaps worse yet become indifferent. I can't do or be all things for all people, as much as I would like. I guess that's Your job? Maybe You can't do it either or maybe we shouldn't? Not sure what I mean or what I'm trying to say here. Just rambling, putting finger to key to see what comes out. Just being me, I guess.

I love You, Dad! I don't say or show it enough, but it's true. I guess I pretty much love everyone, though some are harder to live with or be around. Thank You for the people in my life that show me You, that teach me to love, that teach me about myself and others.

How I love to hear You whisper, "I love you, I'm walking with you! I'm right by your side! I will never hurt you! I will never desert you! I love you my dear child, my dear child!"

I sing those words to myself sometimes. How I long to hear them from your own mouth and see You face to face and give You a hug! I love You, Dad! Don't stop loving me! Your love and the love of those around me sustain me! In the name of the Father and the Son and the Holy Spirit! I love You! Amen!

Another Confession and Prayer

I love you, Father God! Thank you for sticking with me all these years! Thank you for sending Jesus to be my savior and brother and friend! I do not know where this journey of life will lead or how long it will last! Those things are in your keeping! I dream dreams! Wild dreams! But you bring to pass those things that are most helpful. I leave them in your hands! I move forward to write and learn and teach and love! I move forward hopefully, to do your will!

Father God, go with me even as You and Your Son have promised! Dwell with me and in me! Below and above and round about me! To lead and guide and encourage and love! Cast out all fear! Protect and perfect me with your perfect love! Give me courage in you! Teach me to trust you! I do not know if I will emerge alive from this pit of lions, this fiery furnace, we call life, but of this I am certain, you are with me! No one has authority or power over me unless you give it! Help me to submit joyfully to your will!

This I believe that God gives and God takes away and that His every thought and action is to love His children and to see them back safely home with Him! I believe that he has the power to resurrect and to save! The power over life and death! I believe that he has conquered death for us! I believe that because Jesus lives, we will live also! I believe that all of life, who we are and what we can do is a gift from God! I believe that the evil one would try to steal it all away from us! I believe that he would cause us to doubt God and his goodness! Cause us to doubt that God has our best interest at heart! I believe that how we live, that our lives and the choices we make, that the things we do, matter! And I believe that God has a plan and a purpose for us!

Today with God's help and by and in his grace, I chose courage! I chose love and joy and laughter and hope! I choose life! I chose all that is good! And as God gives me strength, I will live it out in my life!

We serve a great God who is worthy of thanks and praise! Therefore, I thank You! Therefore, I praise you, oh God! Your love is amazing! You are God of God, loving Father and kind Brother, Savior, and Friend! I do not fully know You, but the light of Your love and goodness shines in the darkness! Let it shine brightly in us and through us!

You are a great God! Greatly to be thanked and praised! Let all the people praise you, oh God! Let all those you have made, rejoice greatly in you, and in your wonderful and awesome name! For you are YAHWEH! The great I AM! The one in whom all things live and move and have their being! You make all things new and wonderful! You make us whole and one in you! In you there is hope! In you there is joy! In you there is the fullness and abundance of life!

Go with us this day! Dwell in us and round about us! Sanctify and consecrate our every thought, word, and action! Mercifully forgive and restore us when we stumble and fall short! God of God and Light of Light, Hope of all the living, shine in us and through us and round about us! That all may see Your light and come to it! You are God alone! In You there is light and life, love and joy and peace!

Be Thou our light and our life! Love us and lead us and cause us to follow in Your way! For, You are the way, the truth, and the life! We love You, Abba Father! For you first loved us and gave us life in and through Your Son by the power of Your Holy Spirit! Come, Lord Jesus, come! Come, Abba Father, come! Come Holy Spirit, counselor from on high, come! Come and go with us, for we have a message to bring! We have acts of kindness, compassion, and love to perform! Amen and Amen! In Jesus Name Amen!

God-Man Walking

I saw God walking today as a little child,
I saw God walking today as an old man bent and grey,
I saw God walking today as a young man full of life,
I saw God walking today as a beautiful woman,
I saw God walking and working today,
In the kindness of those around me!

A Song for Anna, Michael and Brent

Father let me hear Your voice, for I feel so very alone!
Let Your words fall like gentle rain; let them revive my soul!
Restore my joy!
For I'm lonely and in despair! I don't know where else to turn! Forgive my sins; take away my depression; lift my spirit again!
Draw me to You!

The nights are dark; the days are long! And I just can't go on!
So, please, Father, hear my cry!
Give me hope and strength to carry on!
I need Your help!
Oh, can't You hear me? Have You turned away from me?
Father, are You there?
If You are listening, then let me hear You! Let me know You care!
Let me know You're there!

Then these words were placed upon my heart,
Words He spoke from the very start.
He said, "I have called you as my very own; sealed you with the sign
of the cross! You're redeemed by Christ!
And "I love you! I'm walking with you! I'm right by your side!
I will never desert you! I'll never hurt you!
I love you, my dear child, my dear child!"

And when the nights are dark and days are long,
And you think you're left all alone,
Through the stillness listen for my voice, I'll be singing this song,
"I love you! I'm walking with you! I'm right by your side!
I will never desert you! I'll never hurt you!
I love you, my dear child, my dear child!"

And when the fight is fierce, the battle hard,
And you think there's no way to win!
Don't listen to the battle's din, but to the still voice within, saying
"I love you! I'm walking with you! I'm right by your side!
I will never desert you! I'll never hurt you!
I love you, my dear child, my dear child!"

And when your sight is growing dim,
And the night is falling fast,
Know that I am very close! I'll stay with you until it's past!
"I love you! I'm walking with you!
I'm right by your side!
I will never desert you! I'll never hurt you!
I love you, my dear child, my dear child!"

Then, when that bright new day fully dawns!
And you see me face to face!
I'll wipe away every tear from your eyes.

At last, you have won the race!
And you'll know, I love you! I've been walking with you!
Even living inside! Now there's no more crying! No more dying!
I love you, my dear child, my dear child!

So, go in peace my little one,
For your time has not yet come!
But be certain of my love for you! Because this is most certainly true!
"I love you! I'm walking with you! I'm right by your side!
I will never desert you! I'll never hurt you!
I love you, my dear child, my dear child!"

We thank You, Father God, for answering every prayer!
And sending Your dear Son to die,
And rise, that we might be one! One in Christ!
And we love You! Help us always walk with You! Be thou, our guide!
Grant us joy for the journey!
We rejoice in Your presence! Lead us home to You! We trust in You!

For You love us! You deign to dwell within us!
You call us Your dear child!
You fill us with purpose! Your grace sustains us!
In You, we will abide! What amazing love!
For You love us! You're walking with us, right by our side!
You will never desert us! You will never hurt us!
You love us as Your child, Your dear child!

> **I am with you and will watch over you wherever you go, and I will bring you back to this land. (Genesis 28:15a NIV)**
>
> **Have I not commanded you? Be strong and courageous. Do not be afraid; do not be discouraged, for the Lord your God will be with you wherever you go." (Joshua 1:9 NIV)**
>
> **… And surely I am with you always, to the very end of the age." (Matthew 28:20 NIV)**

Know-One

I met a god one day, Know-One was His Name.
Know-One came to say, Know-One came to pray.
If you but know the Son, one day you'll know the One.
But Know-One came, and no one came.

> **The true light that gives light to everyone was coming into the world. He was in the world, and though the world was made through him, the world did not recognize him. He came to that which was his own, but his own did not receive him. Yet to all who did receive him, to those who believed in his name, he gave the right to become children of God—... (John 1:9-12 NIV)**

> **Jesus answered, "I am the way and the truth and the life. No one comes to the Father except through me. If you really know me, you will know my Father as well. From now on, you do know him and have seen him." Philip said, "Lord, show us the Father and that will be enough for us." Jesus answered: "Don't you know me, Philip, even after I have been among you such a long time? Anyone who has seen me has seen the Father.... (John 14:6-9 NIV)**

Echoes of the Lost

I wonder if anyone cares?
Dares to care -
Cares for the little ones -
-the ones for whom no one cares?

Let me be one with Know-One (no one)!
I AM (i am) is his name!
I AM (i am) Know-One (no one)!
But Know-One (no one) cares!
I Am (i am) one who cares!
For the ones –
For whom -
Know-One (no one) cares!

Children of the Wind

A child's heart sees flowers where only dandelions grow.
A child's heart sees safety in the arms of fearful parents.
A child's heart loves, unconditionally.
A child's heart is content in being.
Lord, help me to see weeds as wildflowers, children as precious gifts.

Learn from the dandelion, you who would be wise.
For where it's seeds land, there it grows, tenacious and persistent. And though most would call it a worthless weed, it knows that it is a beautiful flower. And when its bloom has faded, its life is not spent, instead it is carried in the wind.

> **See! The winter is past; the rains are over and gone. Flowers appear on the earth; the season of singing has come, the cooing of doves is heard in our land. (Song of Songs 2:11-12 NIV)**

> **... "Prophesy to the breath; prophesy, son of man, and say to it, 'This is what the Sovereign Lord says: Come, breath, from the four winds and breathe into these slain, that they may live.'"**
> **(Ezekiel 37:9 NIV)**

> **The wind blows wherever it pleases. You hear its sound, but you cannot tell where it comes from or where it is going. So it is with everyone born of the Spirit. (John 3:8 NIV)**

Any Less

Would you love me any less if... I was not all you claimed me to be?
If my conception happened like any other, perhaps illegitimate in origin or perhaps my mother was the victim of incest or rape?

Would you love me any less if... I was just a man, like any other man?
If I was conceived in sin, and my life was less than perfect?

Would you love me any less if... I was mentally disturbed, - manic depressive or schizophrenic – a victim of my own delusions of grandeur? If my miracles were just some freakish gift, or myths made up, passed on and exaggerated through the ages?

Would you love me any less if ... my eating and drinking got out of hand on occasion – if the rumors of me being a glutton and an alcoholic were true? If I knew prostitutes in "the biblical way" or if one of my disciples was more than just a friend?

Would you love me any less if ... I died, but never rose? If I was the criminal, they made me out to be?

Would you? Should you ... Love me any less?
Would I be any less a precious child of God?

AND if I am all that you claim me to be ...
Would you love them any less? Would you? Should you... love them any less? –
"For I tell you that whatever you have done unto the least of these ... you have done it unto Me."

Oh, Generous Father

You, oh Father, are a God of abundance! You, oh Father, give freely to Your children! Those who trust in You, lack no good thing! Those who trust in You, will reap a harvest of blessing!
Therefore, I will cry out to You and bring to You my cares and concerns! I will lift up the needs of the poor and homeless!

Who can out-give God?

Therefore, I will open my wallet to the poor! I will give, that they may have food! Open the hearts of Your people, that they may care for

Your broken ones! That they may give and not hold back! Therefore, I will open my wallet and give!
I will give my words and my dollars as seed to be planted, that You may bring a harvest in my life and in the lives of the poor! I will give my fish and bread, that multitudes may be fed!

Pour out Your blessings on us! Give to us from Your infinite abundance! Teach us to love! Give, that we may give!
Fling open wide the doors to Your storehouse, that there may be food and healing in the land! Heal those weak in body, and spirit! Enrich those poor in body and soul!! Increase our faith! Increase our joy! Increase our hope! Heal our hearts and multiply our love!

Who will Speak Up

We heard the Palm Sunday Gospel today of Jesus' triumphal entry into Jerusalem. We also heard the lesson of Jesus' trial before Pilate. I couldn't help but wonder what would have happened if all those people who proclaimed Jesus as King on Palm Sunday had spoken up and done the same at Jesus' trial on Good Friday? Or what if Pilate had just kept with his first impressions and refused to crucify the Christ?

I think God is often looking for His people to speak out! All too often though we remain silent! I'm resolving to speak up! Even if it's not popular! Maybe God is waiting for you to speak up too!

> **Speak up for those who cannot speak for themselves, for the rights of all who are destitute. Speak up and judge fairly; defend the rights of the poor and needy. (Proverbs 31:8-9 NIV)**

Lost Song

Lost song, hidden song, in my heart and mind,
Waiting for the right time, again to paint your rhyme.
Lost song, secret song, mingled with despair,

Lost songs, captive notes, one day will fill the air.
And a new song will sound forth, with heart and soul and voice!
A song written before time began! Renewed in time without end!

> ***By the rivers of Babylon we sat and wept when we remembered Zion. There on the poplars we hung our harps, for there our captors asked us for songs, our tormentors demanded songs of joy; they said, "Sing us one of the songs of Zion!" How can we sing the songs of the LORD while in a foreign land?***
> ***(Psalms 137:1-4 NIV)***

Will It Really Make a Difference?

What drives me periodically to this computer to write? What drives me to try and give order to the chaos that is my mind? To pen words in hopes that someone will care, notice, learn, or connect with me (perchance to even pay someday for the privilege of reading)?

The process is too slow, hindered even more by my poor typing abilities! Yet I peck away, in need of a good editor to put in the commas, break up the run-on sentences, and correct the horrendous spelling and grammar! I desire, I suppose, to give meaning to life! Meaning to my life and the lives of others! And to somehow make it more permanent, by putting pen to paper or fingers to keys, as the case may be!

Vanity of vanities, it's all gone in a flash! But perhaps, if it's written down. some legacy will linger! Perhaps the world will be transformed in some small way into a kinder more caring place! Into a universe where people don't go hungry or homeless, where help and not hurt is the norm, and where people love and care for one another despite their differences!

> ***Do not fret because of those who are evil or be envious of those who do wrong; for like the grass they will soon wither, like green plants they will soon die away. Trust in the Lord and do good; dwell in the land and enjoy safe pasture. Take delight in the Lord, and he will give you the desires of your heart. Commit your way to the Lord;***

trust in him and he will do this: He will make your righteous reward shine like the dawn, your vindication like the noonday sun. (Psalm 37:1-6 NIV)

Peter's Call

Oh Father, I do love You! Yes, You know I do!
But more time than Peter, I have denied You too!
Misused Your name and change You,
To the way, I would have You be!
Oh Father, please forgive me! Give me eyes that see!
See You just the way You are, nothing more nor less!
And grant me true perspective on this earthly mess!
So that trusting in You fully, I too may feed Your sheep,
No longer giving my good shepherd, any cause to weep!

> **The third time he said to him, "Simon son of John, do you love me?" Peter was hurt because Jesus asked him the third time, "Do you love me?" He said, "Lord, you know all things; you know that I love you." Jesus said, "Feed my sheep. (John 21:17 NIV)**

Humanity Discovered (Babel Revisited)

In pastures green, where little birds fly,
On wings of seraphs - on wings to die!
Oh Lord, we didn't mean to kill them!
To lay them in the dirt -
To destroy Your creation -
Or cause any hurt!
We only sought to be like God,
Wielding power and flame!
We didn't realize that with power,
Also comes the pain!
So, this time around as we walk the fields –
Let us do so with marvel and with wonder!
Content only to be a part, and not to lay asunder!

The wolf will live with the lamb, the leopard will lie down with the goat, the calf and the lion and the yearling together; and a little child will lead them. The cow will feed with the bear, their young will lie down together, and the lion will eat straw like the ox. The infant will play near the cobra's den, and the young child will put its hand into the viper's nest. They will neither harm nor destroy on all my holy mountain, for the earth will be filled with the knowledge of the Lord as the waters cover the sea. In that day the Root of Jesse will stand as a banner for the peoples; the nations will rally to him, and his resting place will be glorious. (Isaiah 11:6-10 NIV)

<u>Faith and Fertilizer</u>

Have you ever noticed how mountains, and valleys sit side by side?
So too, great faith and doubt, in one person can reside.
But faith's the better friend; more fun to be around.
Content in mountains and valleys, and on the plains, I've found.

Doubt, on the other hand, is never satisfied!
There's always something better, but doubt's afraid to try!
For doubt has no initiative, unless perhaps it's fear!
So, even if doubt accomplishes, it never draws one near...
To God or self or others, doubt always separates!
For no doubt, doubt is common ground, but doubt cannot relate!
Doubt piled high is useless; it really begins to reek...
But add a little air and it generates some heat!
When it's cool and composted, its fertilizer, you know!

But is it really necessary, for true faith to grow?

> *Consider it pure joy, my brothers and sisters, whenever you face trials of many kinds, because you know that the testing of your faith produces perseverance. Let perseverance finish its work so that you may be mature and complete, not lacking anything. If any of you lacks wisdom, you should ask God, who gives generously to all without finding fault, and it will be given to you. But when you ask, you must believe and not doubt, because the one who doubts is like a wave of the sea, blown and tossed by the wind. That person should not expect to receive anything from the Lord. Such a person is double-minded and unstable in all they do. (James 1:2-8 NIV)*

Chess Board Analogies

Sometimes I feel like a pawn – With no value of my own. A piece to be moved about, to be sacrificed to win the match! But Jesus was Your fate any better?

"Checkmate!" the devil cried!

"Alas, I think you're mistaken, but go ahead and try! Try to take me if you will, but look again, you'll see, you're the one in checkmate, for Jesus died for me!"

Perhaps I am a pawn, but if that is what I am, at least I'm on the master's team, and not in Satan's hand. My God is faithful, true and just - He has not deserted me - He sent His Son to be a pawn - A pawn like you and me! But when this chess game is ended, and I reach the end of the board, this lowly pawn will become a king to be sacrificed no more!

So here I am, Lord, make Your play - Use me as You will.
I trust You always - I trust You still!
I trust You, but Lord, I'm frail!

> **Trust in the Lord with all your heart and lean not on your own understanding; in all your ways submit to him, and he will make your paths straight. (Proverbs 3:5-6 NIV)**
>
> **Your kingdom is an everlasting kingdom, and your dominion endures through all generations. The Lord is trustworthy in all he promises and faithful in all he does. The Lord upholds all who fall and lifts up all who are bowed down. (Psalm 145:13-14 NIV)**

Computer Comparisons

My computer is a magnificent machine,
Quite unfathomable to me.
I type some words, then as if by magic,

They appear upon my screen.
How they go from keyboard, to CPU, to screen, to disk,
It is really quite a mystery not unlike our relationship!
For I offer up my prayers, and You communicate with me,
But the connections are quite nebulous,
And so often do I see...
Those annoying little error messages...
Oh, help me Lord to be -
All that You would make me; just print it on my screen.
But Father, don't forget to save it...
To the hard disk.
Put it on the desktop, where it's impossible to miss.
No, No! BIOS is the place it ought to be,
So that every single action will be guided then by thee.
Indeed, it's quite mysterious - What all it takes to make it work!
But one thing is for certain, it's simply not a quirk.
For computers just don't happen, that's quite plain to see.
Likewise, human beings don't just happen to be.
No, You made me as You wanted me, now program me as You see fit!
Configure each and every part, synchronize each byte and bit.
Then I'll be as You designed me, not just a magnificent machine,
But one of God's own children, a living, loving, being!

> **See what great love the Father has lavished on us, that we should be called children of God! And that is what we are!... (1 John 3:1 NIV)**

Eden Reopened

The doorway to the garden of my heart is a tomb,
A cavern cleared of debris and eroded from solid stone.
A tree stands in the garden.
A bud sprouts from the tree,
Stem and leaf, a fragile bloom,
Watered and nurtured by the body and blood of my dead brother;
His Spirit lives in the garden!

The gentle breeze blows through the garden,
The blossom bears fruit,
And a cross-shaped seed is carried on the wind.
The wind blows until it extinguishes the flaming sword;
Until the marauding messenger is put to flight.
Then the seed settles amidst the rubble and ashes;
The ground turns red;
The wind blows harder;
My Father cries!
His tears fall upon a heart-shaped stone.
Sometimes slowly,
Sometime overnight,
The stone is washed away until there is a cavern, an empty tomb.
And the tree begins to grow.

> **After he drove the man out, he placed on the east side of the Garden of Eden cherubim and a flaming sword flashing back and forth to guard the way to the tree of life. (Genesis 3:24 NIV)**
>
> **Then the angel showed me the river of the water of life, as clear as crystal, flowing from the throne of God and of the Lamb down the middle of the great street of the city. On each side of the river stood the tree of life, bearing twelve crops of fruit, yielding its fruit every month. And the leaves of the tree are for the healing of the nations. No longer will there be any curse. The throne of God and of the Lamb will be in the city, and his servants will serve him. They will see his face, and his name will be on their foreheads. There will be no more night. They will not need the light of a lamp or the light of the sun, for the Lord God will give them light. And they will reign for ever and ever. (Revelation 22:1-5 NIV)**

True Abundance

What can I say, I love You, Dad! And You love me!
Someday we'll get there and then I'll see,
Everything so plain it's funny,
I'll wonder why I was so concerned with money -

For life beyond measure is what You offer,
It matters not what's in the coffer!

> *I was young and now I am old, yet I have never seen the righteous forsaken or their children begging bread. (Psalm 37:25 NIV)*

> *Keep your lives free from the love of money and be content with what you have, because God has said, "Never will I leave you; never will I forsake you." (Hebrews 13:5 NIV)*

Show Us Yourself

Oh Lord, have mercy!
Oh Father, love me!
My friend, be my friend!
Do the titles that we use for You,
Say anything about our relationship to You.
Father – I am Your child.
Lord – I am Your slave.
Friend - You are closer than a brother.
Jesus – I am saved.
Yahweh - He is therefore I am.
Do the titles that we use for You,
Say anything about our relationship to You

> *To the faithful you show yourself faithful, to the blameless you show yourself blameless, to the pure you show yourself pure, but to the devious you show yourself shrewd. (Psalm 18: 25-26)*

> *I no longer call you servants, because a servant does not know his master's business. Instead, I have called you friends, for everything that I learned from my Father I have made known to you. You did not choose me, but I chose you and appointed you so that you might go and bear fruit—fruit that will last—and so that whatever you ask in my name the Father will give you. This is my command: Love each other. (John 15:15-17)*

I Am

I am – Yahweh!
I am - what a name!
Do You mind if I borrow it?
Not in a blasphemous sort of way,
But because, Lord, sometimes…
It would just be nice to be-to be me, with all my faults and facets!
Just to be I am!
Not God, but me – I am!
If I mutter heresies, then Father, please, forgive me, but free me also,
Lord, to be the "I am," that Know-One (no-one) sees!

> **Love never fails. … Now I know in part; then I shall know fully, even as I am fully known. (1 Corinthians 13:8, 12b NIV)**

Give Us Godly Impatience, Wisdom and Courage

It's Friday, 7:10 am. I don't have to go into work tonight, so I'm free to get up, knowing that I can sleep later if I want to. I've been caught in a vicious cycle, an endless cycle of hope and despair, of being content and of wanting more, of following dreams and settling, of idealism and facing seeming realities, of scarcity and abundance, of working a job and wanting to work for myself, of wanting to try and of giving up, of walking humbly and trying to fly, of wanting to live and wanting to die, of working hard and hardly working, of sinner and saint!

I get so tired of being tossed about by every wave and thought! Swimming one way then another, never seeming to get anywhere! Just when I'm going well in one direction, I turn around or try to swim in both directions at once! Torn apart by the waves and afraid of the sharks that may or not be there! The best I can do is tread water! Is it a bipolar curse or am I just a slow learner?

I wrote those words almost a week ago. The weekend deteriorated into tears and despair. I feared I was going into a major depression. I wouldn't have given you even money that I would have lasted the week at work. But God is gracious, and Linda is patient and here I am on Thursday and in much better spirits. Will it last or will the weekend bring more despair? I don't know. I think I'm doing well, then WHAM!

I would like to find some type of business or work I can do from home. Sometimes I'm content to keep working until I find it and some days, I'm just ready to quit! When I want to quit it creates a great deal of turmoil, because I know we need the money and I know how I've looked and tried things at home before without success!

What I think I want to do is encourage people to love and care for one another! To forgive one another! To speak the words "I love you!" to one another! To teach people to deal honestly and mercifully with one another! To encourage people to help the poor and the hungry! To encourage them to be grateful, to be generous, and to find ways to improve the world! I want them to trust in God and His precious Son! I want them to live in Him! To live the abundant life, He gives! To love God and love all people! I want those things for others and for myself!

I just don't know how best to do all that and I don't know how to make a living doing that either!

Be patient with us Father and teach us to be patient with ourselves! But at the same time, give us a little Godly impatience and lead us to move ahead, trusting in You!

> *Have I not commanded you? Be strong and courageous. Do not be afraid; do not be discouraged, for the Lord your God will be with you wherever you go." (Joshua 1:9 NIV)*

> *Let the morning bring me word of your unfailing love, for I have put my trust in you. Show me the way I should go, for to you I entrust my life. (Psalm 143:8 NIV)*

Taste and See

Sometimes, yes sometimes, life doesn't rhyme,
But sometimes it does, and then it's, oh so fine!
So good, that you can taste it!
Taste of God and see He is good! Taste of life and know His love!
Oh Lord, at last peace I find, in knowing my true relationship!
I am Your child, nothing more nor less!

> **See what great love the Father has lavished on us, that we should be called children of God! And that is what we are!...(1 John 3:1 NIV)**

Healing Light! - Mixed Metaphors: My High School English Teacher Would Not Approve

Light frightens us! It sounds strange, but it's true! We would rather hide in darkness, than to come into the presence of the light. There is a kind of comfort in darkness, and we fool ourselves into believing that we cannot be seen.

It is better, though, initially more painful, to come into the presence of the light, to let it illuminate the soul and expose every evil and ugly thing that hides there! To expose every hurt, all the pain, the illness, the anger! It is better, to be honest with God and to let Him work His healing! To let Him cut where needed, and bandage and bind up wounds, to even let Him re-break bones, that they may finally heal properly!

It is a frightening and painful process, akin to major surgery! Indeed, we must die on the table, so that God can bring us back to life! It's not just one surgery either, but a series of daily procedures, some more painful than others! Sometimes it is bed rest, sometimes a soothing salve or physical therapy! Sometimes a wound must be cauterized, a cancer excised, or a complete organ transplanted!

But... If we let the light do His work, then we are constantly being healed and transformed into His likeness!

Let us love the light, Father! For though it may bring pain, it is the pain of healing! Darkness brings only our ultimate destruction!

> *The true light that gives light to everyone was coming into the world. He was in the world, and though the world was made through him, the world did not recognize him. He came to that which was his own, but his own did not receive him. Yet to all who did receive him, to those who believed in his name, he gave the right to become children of God—children born not of natural descent, nor of human decision or a husband's will, but born of God. (John 1:9-13 NIV)*

Unashamed

My soul is laid bare, with all its faults! I stand unashamed of the gospel of Christ! I have not labored in vain for my life here has been richer for knowing Him and I hold on to a firm hope for even greater eternal riches to come!

> *What, then, shall we say in response to these things? If God is for us, who can be against us? He who did not spare his own Son, but gave him up for us all—how will he not also, along with him, graciously give us all things? Who will bring any charge against those whom God has chosen? It is God who justifies. Who then is the one who condemns? No one. Christ Jesus who died—more than that, who was raised to life—is at the right hand of God and is also interceding for us. Who shall separate us from the love of Christ? Shall trouble or hardship or persecution or famine or nakedness or danger or sword? As it is written: "For your sake we face death all day long; we are considered as sheep to be slaughtered."*
> *No, in all these things we are more than conquerors through him who loved us. For I am convinced that neither death nor life, neither angels nor demons, neither the present nor the future, nor any powers, neither height nor depth, nor anything else in all creation, will be able to separate us from the love of God that is in Christ Jesus our Lord. (Romans 8:31-39 NIV)*

> *For I am not ashamed of the gospel, because it is the power of God that brings salvation to everyone who believes… (Romans 1:6 NIV)*

> *Jesus performed many other signs in the presence of his disciples, which are not recorded in this book. But these are written that you may believe that Jesus is the Messiah, the Son of God, and that by believing you may have life in his name. (John 20:30-31 NIV)*

To ponder, journal and/or perhaps share:

1. Describe a family dinner you remember, where there was plenty of food and plenty of leftovers.

2. What's one thing that's better as leftovers?

3. What is your earliest memory of Jesus/God? How have your views of God changed over the years? What would you like to reclaim from those early memories?

4. Can you remember a situation where God provided an abundance of resources, when it looked like there might not be enough? If so, describe it.

5. Do you agree with Psalm 37:25? Why or why not?

6. To what can you compare God? Why?

7. Of these leftovers, which is your favorite? Why?

8. Which of these leftovers is your least favorite? Why?

9. What words do you long to hear from God?

10. Have you ever been ashamed of God/Jesus or to admit that you know Him? If so, what caused that?

Images Created by Karlie

Created with a Pixabay Image from Free-Photos

Created with two Pixabay Images from Hans and from Clker-Free-Vector-Images

Created with a Pixabay Image from geralt

Created with a Pixabay Image from ArtsyBee

Chapter Eleven

Overflow Since the First Edition

"The threshing floors will be filled with grain; the vats will overflow with new wine and oil." (Joel 2:24)

"May my lips overflow with praise, for you teach me your decrees. May my tongue sing of your word, for all your commands are righteous." (Psalm119: 171-172 NIV)

Almost six years have passed since clicking the publish button on the first edition. By God's grace the world has kept turning and I have kept writing. They have not been easy years, either for the world or for me personally, but they have not been without joy. The world is still full of heartache and pain; hatred and evil often seem to run rampant! Shootings, bombings, war, famines, fires, hurricanes, earthquakes, and a host of man-made and "natural" disasters seem to daily threaten our continued survival! Most recently the Corona Virus has disrupted our lives. Such things sometimes bring out the worst in people, sometimes the best! Often the best in people and the good things in our world get lost in all the rest. These events as well as more personal ones such as eye troubles, bouts with afib and bradycardia, a pacemaker, back and knee troubles, aging in general, a move to a new home, a new granddaughter, and countless other daily sorrows and joys often cause me to write and reflect. Much of this reflection is contained within the pages of my journal, but some of it has overflowed onto the pages of this book. Most of that overflow is found in this chapter, the rest is scattered throughout the book. These selections range from lighthearted to soulful and serious. I hope they are insightful and helpful!

Oh Spirit Flame

Burn brightly on, Spirit Flame!
Burn brightly and light the world with your love and compassion!
Burn brightly within us!
Light our way and shine your love into the world!

> *"Arise, shine, for your light has come, and the glory of the Lord rises upon you... the Lord rises upon you... Nations will come to your light, and kings to the brightness of your dawn...*
> *(Isaiah 60:1-3 NIV)*

> *"You are the light of the world. A town built on a hill cannot be hidden. Neither do people light a lamp and put it under a bowl. Instead they put it on its stand, and it gives light to everyone in the house. In the same way, let your light shine before others, that they may see your good deeds and glorify your Father in heaven."*
> *(Matthew 5:14-16 NIV)*

Let's Make it a Good Day

I love you Father! You are a great Dad, a great God!
Help me to better know and love you and all the brothers and sisters!
Go with me this day! I know you already promised too!
Help me to follow your lead! We have good to do!
People to minister to and help and love and just be with!

The days are dark...
Help me to shine your love and your light into people's lives!
I love you Dad! I love you Jesus! I love you good Spirit!
Thanks for loving me! Let's make it a good day!

Today

Today!
What a gift! 24 hours, 1440 minutes, 86,400 seconds…
To live in your grace!
To live and laugh and love and cry!
To try and fail and try again and perhaps succeed!
To hope! And hope some more!
To light candles and power on floodlights in a too often dark world!
God grant it and bless it and multiply our humble efforts;
Our often, meager efforts to make a difference!
Yes, multiply them and make a difference…
Exceedingly, abundantly far more than we can think or hope or dream or imagine! For to you great Father-God, I Am of all that is, we commit this day! Together let's make it count for good and for eternity! Amen and Amen! In Jesus Name, Amen!

Each New Day

Another day of your grace and love,
Another day to spend frivolously or wisely,
To waste and squander or to invest!
A day to check off mundane tasks, and to take action on our dreams!
Give plan and focus and structure to this day!
Give us also a spirit of adventure!
Keep us open to spontaneity, variety, and opportunity!
Keep us open to You and to each other!
Thy kingdom come! Thy will be done!
In us and through us and round about us!
As we journey with you on this adventure we call, a new day!

> **"Commit your way to the Lord; trust in him and he will do this: He will make your righteous reward shine like the dawn, your vindication like the noonday sun. Be still before the Lord and wait patiently for him; do not fret when people succeed in their ways, when they carry out their wicked schemes. (Psalm 37: 5-7)**

> *"But encourage one another daily, as long as it is called "Today..." "*
> *(Hebrews 3:13a NIV)*

Poems

Poems are birthed like children often through pain, most full of hope!

Some are conceived quite intentionally, others just seem to happen! Perhaps they are discovered unexpectedly amidst the pages of a journal, or written without fanfare or foreplay, while just fooling around! For some, the pregnancy, labor, and birth are long and tedious! Others are ready to fall upon the delivery room floor, long before they're due! Some spring forth perfect, and full-term! While others are premature births and must be nurtured and cared for in the incubators of heart, soul, and mind, or nursed to health through reams of paper and multiple rewrites!

Most are cherished, at least by those close to them! Some have fame and fortune cast almost immediately upon them! While the beauty and worth of others are only recognized with time! Some are still-born only to be treasured in tears by those who birthed them!
And many are miscarried almost before they were conceived, mere words and phrases, perhaps scrawled in a notebook, or just fading in the mind!

Poems are birthed like children, often through pain, most full of hope! And regardless of their fate...
Whether destined for mediocrity, obscurity, or greatness...
All hold a special place within their creator's heart!

> **"Can a mother forget the baby at her breast and have no compassion on the child she has borne? Though she may forget, I will not forget you! See, I have engraved you on the palms of my hands;...**
> **(Isaiah 49:15-16 NIV)**

No One Reads Poetry Much Anymore

No one, well perhaps a few, reads poetry much anymore!
And I must admit that I too, would rather write it, than read it,
Most days anyway. (Hypocrite that I am!)
So why do I write poetry if so few read it?
Some days it just springs forth! Some days I just get the itch!
It bares my feelings and soul!
It helps me to get in touch with myself at my core!
It matters little if in the eyes of others, it is good or bad!
Whether it is truly inspiring and insightful or pure schmaltz!
I write because I am a writer! I write because at least a few will read!
I write, because I may connect with at least a handful of those that do!

From Mundane to Miraculous

Transform the mundane into the miraculous!

Take our everyday tasks and efforts,
The everyday things of this world,
And do amazing things with them!
Transform them into temporal and eternal blessings!
Blessings for myself, my family, and many, many others!
Yes, bless them and perform miracles with them!
Miracles of your love and kindness and goodness!
Miracles of salvation and grace!
Miracles that will one day cause us to marvel!
Miracles that will cause us and all people,
To give You thanks and praise!

Transform the mundane into the miraculous!

Peggy with the Pigtails

I talk with her as we walk to school.
She's always happy, she's really cool!
And sometimes, as we pass in the hall, she smiles!
Peggy with the pigtails and a button nose!
I think she's cute! She's always kind!
I like her laugh and her soft blue eyes!
I think, I have a crush on her!
Whatever that is, I'm only eight!

The boys all say girls have cuties!
But I don't care!
I like Peggy with the pigtails and a button nose!
Her soft blue eyes and her laugh!
She's always happy, she's always kind!
I think she's cute! I think she's cool!
Even if she is a girl!
I definitely have a crush on her!
Whatever that is, I'm only eight!

Tears

Sometimes in the morning or at night or even mid-day, I cry tears!
Tears of laughter and joy, tears of heartache or break,
Tears of anger and frustration, of anxiety and fear!
Tears that question why and that call out, "How long, oh, Lord!"
Tears that cleanse the soul and spirit, the body and emotions!
Tears that call me to strength and courage in you!
Tears that move me to action… or stillness!
Tears that push me forward, one small step on this journey home!
Amen and Amen! In Jesus Name, Amen!

Wendy the Weimaraner

Wendy the Weimaraner, shining silver friend,
Guardian of children, protective to a fault!

Bought for hunting, she was gun-shy!
To her delight, she was relegated to a life of herding children!

The best babysitter!
She would make the rounds after all were asleep.
If something was amiss…
She would tug, and pull mom's covers off,
Until finally, she would come with her!

Once when a friend of my dad's rough-housed too hard,
He found himself pinned to the floor!
Gazing up into a growling grin!

She jumped through a basement window once,
Just to check on us as we played loudly,
Or perhaps it was just to join in!

We could lay on her and love on her, without complaint!
We would have kept her forever… but she bit the neighbor!
I suspect he deserved it!

Mercifully, she was sentenced to life on a farm!
More room to roam! A new batch of kids to love and herd!

Wendy the Weimaraner, shining silver friend,
Guardian of children, protective to a fault!

The 101st Time's the Charm

I learned something new today,
Learned it new for the 100th time!
I learned it this time in a different and deeper way,
As I spiraled back around once more!
I saw it new and fresh with fuller meaning and impact!
And with renewed hope,
That this time it will produce the desired results!
That this time it will sire greater actions!
Or give birth to an enhanced state of being!
Yes, I learned something new,
Learned it today again for the 100th time!
Help me to hold on to it!
To internalize it!
To utilize it to its full potential!
And if needed to learn it new again,
For the 101st time!

Some Friendly Advice to Husbands

I wrote my wife a love poem, my very soul did I bare.
I fashioned it into a card my feelings with her to share,
She read it rather hurriedly or, so it seemed to me,
She said, "Honey, that's quite nice, but I have someplace to be."
I told her good-by, she smiled and said, "I'll see you later!"
And as she left, she added, "While I'm gone…
Could you please, peel a few potatoes?"

Stunned, I sat in silence and all this began to ponder,
I peeled the spuds as asked and then placed them in some water.
I straightened up and took out the trash, then it hit me like brick,
I needed to buy her a gift, yes, that would do the trick!

I searched with care for the perfect gift, my love to proclaim,

I didn't want my grand gesture to come off looking lame.
When I settled on the perfect gem, I had it wrapped with care,
Then waited until after dinner, the package with her to share,
She opened it, admired it and placed it on her hand,
Then almost without hesitation said, "Honey, could you help me wash the pans?"

I was flabbergasted and bewildered at this nonchalant request,
But I bit my tongue and scrubbed the pots with vigor and with zest!
My wife looked very tired, so I hugged her and offered a massage,
She said, "I'm doing fine, but tomorrow could you clean out the garage?"

The next day, it occurred to me,
"More time together is what we need!"
I offered a weekend get-away,
She said, "Could we stay home and trim the trees?"
Disappointed and discourage I headed out the door,
I knew one thing for certain, I couldn't take much more!

I straightened the garage,
Trimmed the trees, then mowed and edged the lawn,
I weeded all the flower beds, till my frustrations were finally gone!
My wife took notice of all my work, hugged and kissed me as a start,
By trial and error and accident,
I had found the key to unlock her heart!

For some its words of affirmation, and others need a gift,
Some like hugs and touch and kisses, to give their heart a lift,
For some time together is the language that they hear,
But for my wife, it's service that shouts, "I love you!" in her ear!

So, gentlemen save yourself some time, I've laid it out very plain,
Take note of your loved-one's language,

Save yourself some time and pain,
But if like me, you're a little slow or just need a second look,
Then don't just take my word for it, read Gary Chapman's book!

My wife's an amazing jewel, the one in Proverbs 31 can't compare!
With greater depth and facets, than the portrait I've painted here!
I'm sure she'll smile and chuckle, when she reads this poem,
Especially, if I've checked off the honey-dos,
And straightened up our home!

> *"Husbands, love your wives, just as Christ loved the church and gave himself up for her…" (Ephesians 5:25 NIV)*
>
> *"Love is patient, love is kind. It does not envy, it does not boast, it is not proud. It does not dishonor others, it is not self-seeking, it is not easily angered, it keeps no record of wrongs. Love does not delight in evil but rejoices with the truth. It always protects, always trusts, always hopes, always perseveres." (1 Corinthians 13:4-7)*

From Defeat, Victory

I wrestled the defending state champion one day,
Many years ago! Many tears ago!
It was akin to wrestling an octopus in a whirlwind,
As move followed upon move, in dizzying succession!
I scored 6 points to his 22, but I didn't get pinned!
They had to carry me off the mat!
I lost 22-6! But saved 2 team points!
My teammates mobbed and cheered me!
You'd have thought I had won!
My two points…Along with an unexpected win by a teammate,
Made the difference! We won the dual meet we were destined to lose!
Oh, that life was more often like that day,
With people cheering valiant efforts, regardless of the outcome!
Picking each other up and spurring each other on to victory!

He died on a cross! On a hill! Many years ago! Many tears ago!

Died in defeat, the battle lost!
But his resurrection gives us the victory!

> **"... let us consider how we may spur one another on toward love and good deeds... encouraging one another—and all the more as you see the Day approaching. (Hebrews 10:24-25 NIV)**

> **" 'He will wipe every tear from their eyes. There will be no more death' or mourning or crying or pain, for the old order of things has passed away." (Revelation 21:4)**

This Thing Called Faith

It's a messy business this thing called faith, called belief, called trust!
Trust seems to sum it up, at least for me!
But trust in what?
Trust in a God we cannot know or hear or see?
Trust in ancient books penned by prophets,
Men led by God or perhaps not?
Trust in the Bible, the Torah, the Koran, the scriptures of the Hindu or Buddhist, or others?
Trust in traditions and teachings handed down through the ages?
Trust in men, holy men, who lived and loved and taught and died?
Imperfect men or perfect men, perhaps a God-Man, who rose again?
Trust in ourselves, in our own thoughts and feelings?
Trust in a conscience?
In a spirit of goodness or hate that dwells within us?
Trust in each other, though we are often unworthy of trust?
Trust in love?
How can we sort it all out?
It's a messy business this trust and belief and faith thing!

> **"Trust in the Lord with all your heart and lean not on your own understanding; in all your ways submit to him, and he will make your paths straight." (Proverbs 3:5-6 NIV)**

...Jesus went into Galilee, proclaiming the good news of God. "The time has come," he said. "The kingdom of God has come near. Repent and believe the good news!" (Mark 1:14-15 NIV)

This Thing Called Hope

What shall I say about this thing called hope?
Hope brightens our day!
It lights our way! "Hope springs eternal!"
And so, perhaps, hope comes from the eternal one?

What shall I say about hope in a world so often filled,
With hate and evil and violence and death and destruction?
I say, that we must hope against all these things!
Hope against hopelessness! Hope in the face of certain death!
Hope in something greater than ourselves!
Greater than this world!
Greater than evil and sin and death and destruction!

Yes, hope in the eternal one! And in His Son!
And in all the people of this sin-stained world,
Who continue to hope and to love and to have faith!

Yes, "hope springs eternal!"
For there is no hope but in the one eternal God!
The source of all hope and goodness; the source of light and love!
And that's all I have to say about hope, for now!

> *"... but those who hope in the Lord will renew their strength. They will soar on wings like eagles; they will run and not grow weary, they will walk and not be faint. (Isaiah 40:31 NIV)*
>
> *"Let us hold unswervingly to the hope we profess, for he who promised is faithful." (Hebrews 10:23 NIV)*
>
> *...In his great mercy he has given us new birth into a living hope through the resurrection of Jesus Christ from the dead, and into an inheritance that can never perish, spoil or fade. (1 Peter 1:2-4 NIV)*

Time Echoes

Saturday – football! Innocent enough! Tommy got up a game!
Just a group of 4th graders having fun, kid's stuff!
All was harmonious...
Until Steve launched a flying block tackle to my back!
I went down hard! The ball erupting out of control!
"Fumble!" someone yelled,
The other team quickly scooped up the ball and ran for a touchdown!

Back on my feet, I cried foul, to no avail!
No referees in this kid's-stuff-game!
Steve pressed his side of the argument! He was in my face!
Then, he punched my face!
I retaliated jabbing, jabbing, landing blow after blow to his jaw!
He swung wide and wild, when he could get one off!
Then a roundhouse out of nowhere, bloodied my nose!
(I bled easily in those days.)
Blood and tears gushing down my face! I continued my onslaught –
Jabbing, jabbing, pommeling his jaw!
Then out of nowhere, Tommy stepped in!

We paused for a moment, posturing, eager to get back at it!
But Tommy persisted! He insisted we break it up!
I looked at Steve and Steve looked at me!
We both looked a Tommy... an athlete among athletes...
With size and stature and strength ...
A formidable presence, beyond his years!
Neither Steve nor I wanted to confront him!
Besides I counted him as my best friend!
So –
We just went home!
Me with my bloody nose! Steve red-faced and sore!
And to my surprise, the game continued!

Monday - back at school… Steve and I smoothed things over.
It was just kid's stuff, after all!
Tommy would have wanted it that way!
I counted him as my best friend!

I moved from there the next year.
I lost track of Steve until high school. He became a Doctor.
I've done a few things.
Now, I babysit granddaughters and smith words.
As for Tommy, we kept in touch.
He invited me over to his house from time to time.
I remember his 13th birthday party, 8th-grade year,
He talked of playing high school ball.
I knew, in time, he'd make the pros!
An athlete among athletes, with size and stature and strength –
A formidable presence and smart!
He had all the tools! I counted him as my best friend!

Then, out of nowhere, a wild roundhouse sent us all reeling!
And meningitis left Tommy dead! At 13! In his 8th grade year!
This was definitely not kid's stuff!
There was no way to smooth it over or make it right!

I cried foul, to no avail!
There were no referees in this vicious, hopeless game of death!
It hit me hard! A flying block tackle from behind!
I ran to my room! I fought back the tears!
But they erupted out of control!

Saturday - funeral - minister proclaiming…
"Tommy loved football! He loved the game!"
What followed 's a blur! Memorial service! Internment! Wake!
All swirling in senselessness and futility!

A flood of emotions gushed through my body - out my eyes –
And down my face!

Still –
Amidst the sorrow, sadness, anger, and pain – there were smiles!
And even laughter – as we remembered and reminisced!
Tommy loved football! Tommy loved life!
I counted him as my best friend!

Then-
We just went home!
Eyes still red and sore! Souls still battered, bloodied, and bruised!
And to my surprise, the game continued!

Monday – school! Tuesday -school! Wednesday – school!
Hope gradually returning!
Saturday - Kids still playing football! Perhaps next week, I'll join in!
Things unfolding as they should!
High school! College! Family and children!

And now-
Steve a Doctor!
And I a Papa, who crafts words!
Tommy would have wanted it that way!
Tommy loved football! He loved the game!
I counted him as my best friend!

But senselessness and futility-
Death! Hunger! And war continue too!
Meningitis! Cancer! And more! – Still take their toll!

And now-
Children kill children! Children kill themselves!
A vicious, hopeless game of death!

It's definitely not kid's stuff!
No way to smooth it over or make it right!
Tommy would not have wanted it that way!

But if the spirit of love and joy, kindness and courage -
Remain a formidable presence within us!
If we step in! If we rise up!
To our full stature, with wisdom and strength!
If we persist! If we insist on change!
If we insist on treating each other with love and respect and care!

Then –
In little ways! And perhaps big!
Anger! Sadness! Fear! And despair! –
Give way! To hope! And action! And life!
Tommy would have wanted it that way!
Tommy loved football! Tommy loved life!
I counted him as my best friend!

Let the game continue!

> **What, then, shall we say in response to these things? If God is for us, who can be against us?... For I am convinced that neither death nor life, neither angels nor demons, neither the present nor the future, nor any powers, neither height nor depth, nor anything else in all creation, will be able to separate us from the love of God that is in Christ Jesus our Lord. (Romans 8 31, 38-39 NIV)**

Intentional Take-Aways from My Time in Therapy in More-or-Less Random Order

Life is meant to be lived! Sometimes life is hard! Be present in the moment! Work for progress not perfection! Keep it simple! Don't be too serious! Beyond a healthy discipline, be gentle with yourself! Small changes when applied consistently over time produce big results! Even with the best preparation, stuff still happens, then we deal with it as best we can with the resources we have at the time! You don't have to wait until Monday to make a change; each day contains multiple opportunities to start fresh if needed! Sometimes you must accept and live with or through your feelings! That which gets measured gets managed! Swimming (exercise) in moderation is helpful! Be intentional about what you do! You can't be all things for all people! Love, laughter, tears, and forgiveness are some of the ingredients of healing! Avoid absolute, catastrophic, and negative thinking patterns! Prayer, praise, gratitude, and forgiveness are integral to my sense of wellbeing!

I am loved by God! He wants the best for me! He is our refuge and our strength, an ever-present help! Rest, regroup, refocus, but never give up!

> *"Come to me, all you who are weary and burdened, and I will give you rest. Take my yoke upon you and learn from me, for I am gentle and humble in heart, and you will find rest for your souls. For my yoke is easy and my burden is light." (Matthew 11:28-30)*

> *"Finally, be strong in the Lord and in his mighty power. Put on the full armor of God, so that you can take your stand against the devil's schemes. For our struggle is not against flesh and blood, but against the rulers, against the authorities, against the powers of this dark world and against the spiritual forces of evil in the heavenly realms. Therefore put on the full armor of God, so that when the day of evil comes, you may be able to stand your ground, and after you have done everything, to stand. Stand firm then..."*
> *(Ephesians 6:10-14a NIV)*

Puya raimondii 'Mike'

Beautiful Bromeliad cultivar!
Bred in the Father's heart and mind!
Nurtured and tended by the spirit of His Son!
And the kindness and care of many others!
60 years for buds to form!

Ready to burst into bloom!
Hopes and prayers abound that this plant,
Will not only bloom with bounty and beauty,
But that perhaps the plant will survive and bloom again and again!
That it will bear delicious and nourishing fruit, filled with many seeds!
Seeds that produce a host of new cultivars and hybrids!
In a multitude of sizes, shapes, and colors!
Plants that grow fast and furious!
Plants that flower and fruit often!
With more glory than their parent!
Plants adapted to a variety of environments!
That thrive and flourish wherever they are planted!
Plants whose fruits nourish the lives of many!
And whose seeds spawn yet another generation of hope!

I Write Schmaltz

I write schmaltz! (or so some say),
Excessive sentimentality, pure rendered chicken fat! (or so some say)
Not only do I write it…but I believe it! (most days anyway)
When I look at the world,
And all the darkness, and hatred and pure unadulterated evil,
I am compelled to believe it…
Or else to live without hope or joy, or love or laughter…
And that would be no life at all!
Besides schmaltz, in good proportion make things taste better!
Bon Appetit!

Boundaries

I suspect, boundaries should be more like "fences" than "walls,"
My boundaries anyway,
Fences "breathe,"
They have "gates" to let others in and out,
To let "good" in and "bad" out!

Walls, especially if they have no gates, hold everything in!
And keep everything out!
The "good" and the "bad!"
Helpful things cannot flow in and hurtful things cannot flow out!
Perhaps your boundaries need to be more wall-like,
At least for a while,
Just to protect yourself or to give yourself time to process and to heal!
But, I hope they at least have gates,
And that you open them, from time to time!

Boundaries, I suspect, should be like skin!
Like membranes, and tissues,
That define the various body parts and allow them to work together!
Membranes that allow life-giving fluid to flow in!
Bringing oxygen and nutrients, and carrying away toxic byproducts,
Before they build up to dangerous levels!
Boundaries, I suspect, should be selectively permeable membranes!

Forgiveness and love, I suspect,
Allow boundaries to not become walls without gates!
They allow membranes to remain permeable!
They allow organs to continue to function and remain healthy parts of the body!

Boundaries, forgiveness, and love are not easy things,
They do not often come naturally, but I suspect, they are necessary!
Necessary for health and healing and wellbeing!
I suspect, boundaries give us the freedom, authority, space and ability,
To let our "Yes" be "Yes" and our "No" be "No!"
The freedom, authority, space and ability to heal,
From all that has caused us hurt or harm!
Boundaries are not easy things for many of us,
But they are good and necessary and important things!
They define us and help us to live and love,

To survive and thrive, in this crazy, often hurtful world!

> *...speaking the truth in love, we will grow to become in every respect the mature body of him who is the head, that is, Christ. From him the whole body, joined and held together by every supporting ligament, grows and builds itself up in love, as each part does its work. (Ephesians 4:15-16 NIV)*

<u>*A Note on the Poem Boundaries:*</u> *The analogies of boundaries as fences and walls in the poem above are from the Book:* <u>*Boundaries: When to Say Yes, How to Say No to Take Control of Your Life*</u> *Copyright ©1992, 2017 by Dr. Henry Cloud and Dr. John Townsend. Though I have not intentionally tried to quote them, some of their words and concepts resonate with me and are echoed in this poem. I gratefully acknowledge their contribution and highly recommend their book.*

Good Father, Help us define and defend our boundaries! Help us do boundaries well!

Protect us from those who would violate our boundaries, and give us courage, authority and voice to defend those boundaries in love! Help us to respect the boundaries of others. Forgive us and help us make amends, when we trespass upon those boundaries.

Teach us to love rightly and to forgive. Help us see and appreciate the boundaries you have ordained, boundaries that make us distinct and vital parts of your body. Boundaries that make us whole and one in you; one body with all the parts working together; One family with all the members loving and caring for and respecting each other!

Help us to do boundaries well, in the here and now and in eternity!

Amen! In Jesus Name! May it be so!

Just for a Day or Two

If I could be you and you could be me just for a day or two...
Would we still have different points of view?
Would we at least learn and comprehend...?
That there is beauty and worth in everyone!
That uniqueness and differences are to be respected and valued!

That we need each other!
That in important ways we are all, alike!
That there is a oneness that makes us brothers and sisters and friends!
Go peacefully and be!
Go peacefully and prosper and live and love and forgive and be kind!

> **"Love must be sincere. Hate what is evil; cling to what is good. Be devoted to one another in love... Do not repay anyone evil for evil. Be careful to do what is right in the eyes of everyone. If it is possible, as far as it depends on you, live at peace with everyone." (Romans 12:9-10a, 17-18 NIV)**

Visiting Ann

Anna Belle is 93, I visit her from time to time,
Though according to her not nearly often enough,
Nor do I ever stay, long enough!
And sometimes my guilty conscience concurs.

Often, I sit next to her and rub her shoulders,
She nods off, I suspect visiting another place and time,
Just where I'm not sure.
If I pause the massage she wakes and complains,
"Don't stop, don't stop!"

Other days we sit and talk,
And I answer the same questions again and again and yet again.
To get relief from the repetition,
I show her pictures and videos on my phone.
She loves the ones of dogs and horses, cats, and kids...
Both human and goat!
Sometimes, I tell her jokes and she laughs!
She's heard them all before...
But they are new to her with each retelling.

Sometimes my wife comes along,
We bring her a protein bar or a diet soda,
She loves chocolate and sweets, but candy raises her blood sugar.
If the weather cooperates, we may venture outdoors...
For walk or just to sit,
Occasionally, we go for a drive...
When we can muster the energy and assistance to get her in and out of the van.

If she is in bed, when we come, we may not stay long.
I sit in her wheelchair and lean near her,
Perhaps, I read her a few Psalms.
The 23rd is here favorite...
She recites it from memory, as I read.
Perhaps before we go, I offer a prayer,
Or we lay her headphones near her,
So, she can listen to her favorite songs and hymns...
Without disturbing her roommate,
We would place them on her head,
But she refuses because "they mess up my hair!"

Anna Belle is 93, I visit her from time to time.

> *... I was hungry, and you gave me food to eat. I was thirsty, and you gave me drink. I was a stranger, and you took me in. I was naked, and you clothed me. I was sick, and you visited me. I was in prison, and you came to me.' (Matthew 25:35-36 WEB)*

Of Love and Lotteries

I dream of winning the lottery, of being wealthy beyond belief!
I dream of all the good things we could do with that money!
The lives and communities of love and hope we could build!
But money changes people! It often brings out the worst in them!
It causes them to trust God less!

I bought a couple of lottery tickets the other day,
Yes, with the hope and a prayer that we might win!
With dreams of all the good we might do with it!
But also praying thy kingdom come, thy will be done!
For often I do not know what is best for myself or others!

Father, help me to realize that you have made me your child and heir,
That I am already wealthy beyond belief!
Wealthy in the things that truly matter in this world and in the next,
Things like love, and joy, like peace amidst trouble and sorrow,
Like faith and hope,
Like patience and perseverance,
Like kindness and goodness,
Like gentleness and faithfulness, and forgiveness!
Yes, I am infinitely rich in these and all things that matter most!
Rich in the gifts you give,
And in the fruit of righteousness and love that you cultivate within us!
Rich in abundant life that transcends time and space and seeming reality!

Help me to draw on these things!
Help me to share these things!
Help me to invest in these things!
Help these things to grow and flourish in my life,
And in the lives of those around us!

And well Father God, if you can throw in a lottery win,
That's just salt or gravy or spice!
And we could do some good with it!
We could season some lives with it!
But you know best good Father! You are the master chef!
You have already prepared a rich banquet for us!
You have already given us a foretaste of the things that are to come,
At the wedding feast of your Son!

You have already prepared for us, wealth and goodness and gladness and unity and community, beyond our wildest dreams!
Therefore, let our trust, our hope, our joy, and our peace be in you!
As we pray, "Thy kingdom come! Thy will be done!"

> *Then Jesus said to his disciples, "Truly I tell you, it is hard for someone who is rich to enter the kingdom of heaven. Again I tell you, it is easier for a camel to go through the eye of a needle than for someone who is rich to enter the kingdom of God." When the disciples heard this, they were greatly astonished and asked, "Who then can be saved?" Jesus looked at them and said, "With man this is impossible, but with God all things are possible."*
> *(Matthew 19:23-26 NIV)*

> *Command those who are rich in this present world not to be arrogant nor to put their hope in wealth, which is so uncertain, but to put their hope in God, who richly provides us with everything for our enjoyment. Command them to do good, to be rich in good deeds, and to be generous and willing to share. In this way they will lay up treasure for themselves as a firm foundation for the coming age, so that they may take hold of the life that is truly life.*
> *(1 Timothy 6:17-19 NIV)*

> *"This, then, is how you should pray: "'Our Father in heaven, hallowed be your name, your kingdom come, your will be done, on earth as it is in heaven. Give us today our daily bread. And forgive us our debts, as we also have forgiven our debtors. And lead us not into temptation, but deliver us from the evil one.'"*
> *(Matthew 6:9-13 NIV)*

Our Jesus

Thy Kingdom Come! Thy Will Be Done!
In us... and through us... and round about us!
As you come to us and comfort us!
As you come to us and confront us!
As you dwell in us and transform us!
As you feed us and forgive us!
As you give us the desire, courage, and ability...
To feed and forgive others!
As we revere you and honor you!

As we treat each other with love and compassion; honor and respect!
As you die for us! And rise for us! And live for us!
As you intercede for us!
As you break the hold of temptation and evil upon us!
And as you walk with us through every trial and temptation!

Thy Kingdom Come! Thy will be done!
In Us… and through us… and round about us!
In the eternal-permanence of your Father's presence!
In our transient but all-too-real earthly existence!
In realms of heaven and earth…which will be made new in eternal glory, magnificence, and reality beyond our ability to comprehend or dream or imagine!
Yes, In the "Now" and the "Not Yet" of time and eternity!
In Spirit and in truth! Thy Kingdom come! Thy will be done!

"Yahweh Saves!"
This name we proclaim! This name we pray!
Amen and Amen!

> **"But in your hearts revere Christ as Lord. Always be prepared to give an answer to everyone who asks you to give the reason for the hope that you have. But do this with gentleness and respect…"**
> **(1 Peter 3:15)**

Number our Days in Love!

Father God, bless and order our days!
And as it is your will and as it is helpful to us and others,
Extend our time in this place!
Your love endures forever!

Keep us ever mindful that you are our Father, our Daddy, our Abba,
Who knows what's best for us and all our dear brothers and sisters!
Your love endures forever!

You have opened paradise and eternity to us!
Therefore, order and number our days as you see fit!
Your love endures forever!

Give us wise and discerning hearts and minds!
Teach us to walk in your ways!
Your love endures forever!

Teach us to live and move and have our being,
In You! In Your Son! In community and unity with one another!
Through Your Spirit!
Make us one!
Your Love endures forever!

Teach us to love and live and forgive!
Your Love endures forever!

Thy kingdom come! Thy will be done! Love us and lead us!
Your Love endures forever!

Good Father of life and love,
Make your works and your ways, our ways!
Your Love endures forever!

Teach us to love and laugh with You!
To make all our requests known to You!
Your Love endures forever!

Order our days!
Increase our hope and love, our joy, and peace!
Let us live productive lives of service and love!
In You and in Your Son, through Your Good Spirit!
Your Love endures forever!

Hallowed be thy name among us!
In Jesus Name! Amen! Amen!
Be thou our yes! The answer to our hearts desire!
Your Love endures forever!

We Can Make a Difference

Sometimes we feel so small in this big crazy world. We feel that our voice and our actions don't matter! We feel that there is nothing we can do to change the violence and evil in this world! Christ warns us that "because of the increase of wickedness, the love of most will grow cold" (Matthew 24:12 NIV) Our challenge is to keep love's fire burning brightly in our hearts and lives and to not let fear or anger or hatred rule our thoughts, words, and actions!

I believe our words and actions do make a difference! I believe that every kind word and action are melodies around which God writes and performs His Opus! They are a chorus for hope and peace! And I believe that God can do exceedingly, abundantly, far more than we think, or hope or dream or imagine!

Therefore, I am determined with God's help, to not let my "love grow cold!" To continue to do good! To continue to encourage others! To continue to speak out for peace! And to spread hope! Join me in God's opus of love, in this chorus for hope and peace. Every voice is important! Every act of kindness and love counts! In every way that you are able, let your love abound more and more! Spread peace! Spread hope! Spread joy! Continue to love! Remain vigilant in prayer!

May everyone of all faiths and those who have turned away from faith call upon God, repenting of their evil and indifferent ways, and may they raise an opus of love and a chorus for hope and peace!

"Therefore we do not lose heart. Though outwardly we are wasting away, yet inwardly we are being renewed day by day. For our light

and momentary troubles are achieving for us an eternal glory that far outweighs them all. So we fix our eyes not on what is seen, but on what is unseen, since what is seen is temporary, but what is unseen is eternal. (2 Corinthians 4:16-18 NIV)

"Grace and peace to you from God our Father and the Lord Jesus Christ, who gave himself for our sins to rescue us from the present evil age, according to the will of our God and Father, to whom be glory for ever and ever. Amen." (Galatians 1:3-5 NIV)

Father,

Let our response to these evil days be neither hatred or indifference! Let the light of your love burn more brightly than before! Increase our love! Increase our faith! Teach us to Love! Teach us to forgive! Grant hope! Grant wisdom! Grant courage! Change hearts! Change minds! Change lives! Draw us to you and to each other! Have mercy on us all!

Dear Father,

Renew my heart and mind, my body, soul, and spirit to love you and those around me. Let me sow seeds of love and mercy, hope, and joy, abundantly into the lives of others, that together we might reap an eternal harvest in you! In Jesus Name, Amen!

I Choose

Trouble may come in this life, but we don't have to invite it in or let it control our lives by negative thinking patterns!

Today with God's help:
I choose joy!
I choose hope!
I choose life!
I choose love!
I choose courage!

We go forth boldly knowing that God works out all things for our ultimate good and the good of others! Thank You, kind Father! Thank You for promising to be with us no matter what comes!

Shalom My Friend!

Shalom, what a word! Peace and joy and health and wellness!
Harmony and wholeness and oneness and completeness!
Community and contentment! Love, prosperity, and more!
Beyond understanding! Beyond seeming reality!
All those things we have in God!
All those things are embodied in Christ!
All those things are ours now!
Even in a world full of their opposites!

Our hello and our good-bye! The holding on and the letting go!
The sorrow and the joy! The near and the far!
The now and not yet! The kingdom of God!
All are encompassed and indwelled,
By the shalom of God! Shalom what a word!

Shalom my Friend!

> **"Shalom" I leave with you. My "Shalom" I give to you; not as the world gives, give I to you. Don't let your heart be troubled, neither let it be fearful. (John 14:27 -Mike's Revised Version based on the WEB)**

Oh, Prince of Peace, Shepherd of Shalom, Father and Savior, Brother, Spirit and Friend, I-Am of all that exists, grant us your shalom! Be thou our shalom!

In Jesus Name! Yahweh saves! Blessed be the name of Yahweh! Shalom and Amen!

To ponder, journal and/or perhaps share:

1. What is one thing you need to do "today"?

2. Whose shoes would it probably be helpful for you to walk in at least for a day or two? Why is that?

3. What are some things you believe or trust in?

4. What are some things that give you hope?

5. Who was your first crush? Why? What did you like about that person?

6. Did you have pets while growing up? If so, what are some of your memories of them?

7. What is the first time you remember someone dying? How did it impact your life?

8. What are some things that you hold dear that others might consider unnecessary or "schmaltz?"

9. Is there someone you should or would like to or call or visit today? Who? Why?

10. What is something in your life that some might call a "defeat" but which you look at as a victory?

11. Who is someone to whom you would like to give some "friendly" advice? What advice would you give and why?

12. What does praying, "Thy kingdom come, Thy will be done" mean for/to you?

13. How well do you do "boundaries?" How well do you define and manage your own? How well do you respect other's boundaries? Are your boundaries more like "fences" or "walls?" Why is that?

14. What "body part" "organ" or "tissue" are you most like? Why? What is one important contribution you make to others?

15. What are some lessons you have learned about life to this point? What are some things you seem to have to learn repeatedly?

16. What is one area of your life that you especially need to experience God's "shalom"?

17. What is one thing you would like to remember and take to heart from this book?

18. Try writing a prayer for yourself, those around you, and/or for the world.

> Trouble may come in this life, but we don't have to invite it in or let it control our life by negative thinking patterns!
>
> Today, with God's help:
> I choose Joy!
> I choose Hope!
> I choose Life!
> I choose Love!
> I choose Courage!
> I go forth boldly knowing that God works all things out for our ultimate good and the good of others!
> Thank You, kind Father! Thank You for promising to be with me no matter what comes!
>
> mikefreed.xyz

Created with a Pixabay Image from geralt

Chapter Twelve

The Doxology

Great is Yahweh (the LORD), and greatly to be praised! His greatness is unsearchable. One generation will commend your works to another, and will declare your mighty acts. Of the glorious majesty of your honor, of your wondrous works, I will meditate. Men will speak of the might of your awesome acts. I will declare your greatness. They will utter the memory of your great goodness, and will sing of your righteousness. Yahweh (the LORD) is gracious, merciful, slow to anger, and of great loving kindness. Yahweh (the LORD) is good to all. His tender mercies are over all his works. All your works will give thanks to you, Yahweh. (LORD) Your saints will extol you. They will speak of the glory of your kingdom, and talk about your power; to make known to the sons of men his mighty acts, the glory of the majesty of his kingdom. Your kingdom is an everlasting kingdom. Your dominion endures throughout all generations. Yahweh (the LORD) is faithful in all his words, and loving in all his deeds. (Psalm 145:3-13 WEB)

(Yahweh was the Hebrew name for God it is most often translated the LORD. These parentheses were added to the text by the book's author.)

Created by Karlie with PicSay Pro

Chapter Thirteen

The Blessing

For this reason I kneel before the Father, from whom every family in heaven and on earth derives its name. I pray that out of his glorious riches he may strengthen you with power through his Spirit in your inner being, so that Christ may dwell in your hearts through faith. And I pray that you, being rooted and established in love, may have power, together with all the Lord's holy people, to grasp how wide and long and high and deep is the love of Christ, and to know this love that surpasses knowledge—that you may be filled to the measure of all the fullness of God.

Now to him who is able to do immeasurably more than all we ask or imagine, according to his power that is at work within us, to him be glory in the church and in Christ Jesus throughout all generations, for ever and ever! Amen. (Ephesians 3:14-21 NIV)

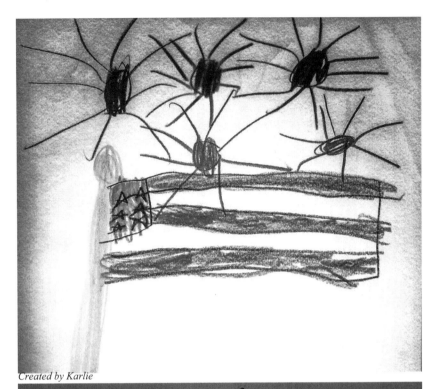

Created by Karlie

Created by Karlie with PicSay Pro

Acknowledgments

"We always thank God for all of you and continually mention you in our prayers. We remember before our God and Father your work produced by faith, your labor prompted by love, and your endurance inspired by hope in our Lord Jesus Christ. For we know, brothers and sisters loved by God, that he has chosen you, because our gospel came to you not simply with words but also with power, with the Holy Spirit and deep conviction..." (1 Thessalonians 1:2-5a)

Many people have impacted my life both positively and negatively. Their words and their actions have shaped my life and are reflected in these pages. To the best of my human ability, I have made peace with them all; forgiving where I felt I had been wronged and when possible, seeking forgiveness and reconciliation with those I have wronged or hurt in some way.

First, I acknowledge God, Father, Son, and Holy Spirit! He has been my constant companion on this journey of life. He refused to desert me, even when I cursed Him! There were many days I would not have made it, had He not carried me! He taught me to love and forgive and to live! So, first and foremost, I acknowledge our great God and His power, presence, and grace in my life!

The Honor Due

What words shall I write to praise Your name?
What words shall I write to proclaim Your fame?
What words shall I write in this dark night?
I will be still, and know You are God!

"... Be still, and know that I am God; I will be exalted among the nations, I will be exalted in the earth." (Psalms 46:10 NIV)

Next, I would like to acknowledge my family, both immediate and extended. My parents, my brother and sisters, my grandparents, aunts and uncles, etc. laid a firm foundation that still supports me today. You are/were great, and I love you!

Likewise, I have been truly blessed to have the wife (Linda) and daughters (Elizabeth and Rebekah) that I do. I am so grateful for their constant love and support. We have since, added a son-in-law, Kevin and granddaughters, Karlie and Maddie to the clan and their presence has enriched our lives in ways too numerous to mention. If that weren't enough, there are in-laws of all kinds, nieces, nephews, great-nieces, great-nephews. great-great nieces and a great-great-nephew. Some we see often, others less often, but all have touched our lives.

Which brings me to my friends, some old, some new, who have been there in good days and bad. I don't know where to begin. I have been so blessed by my friends; friends from youth group, high school and college; my friends and colleagues in ministry; peers, teachers, and mentors from all walks of life. I would list them all by name, but it would take a book in itself and I would surely leave someone out. Some friends I have lost touch with, some touched my life only for a short time and others are seemingly "forever" friends. I love you all! Thanks for being a part of my life!

Blessed is the One

With ears that do not burn when the word's run hot,
With hands that sift them,
And lips that blow or if needed burn the chaff away,
Exposing only grain.
With arms that comfort,
And feet that walk along beside.
With an understanding gaze,
And a forgiving heart.
One who will laugh with you, cry with you,

Perchance to even die for you.
Blessed is the one who has such a friend!

Morning Words

Oh, Father, night falls and darkness calls and in the morning, I write,
For words hidden in darkness, never bring any light.
But words shared with a compassionate friend,
Be they darkness or light,
Are words that build, words that heal!
Words that keep us through the night!

> ***A friend loves at all times, and a brother is born for a time of adversity. (Proverbs 17:17 NIV)***

I would especially like to acknowledge my brother, Steve for his words of encouragement and for letting me use his poem as the foreword to this book. Many thanks go to my friends and relatives who have read, help edit, and commented on various versions of the work as it progressed and to Karlie and Mykayla for adding their artistic touches. A special thanks to my former psychologist, Melissa who helped turn my life around; the input and ponderings from many of our sessions are reflected in this book.

Finally, to all the people I have hurt or harmed, either intentionally or unintentionally, I ask your forgiveness. I'm sure there are many, but for some reason, these come to mind; a girl I left on the dance floor in high school, because I wanted to dance the last dance with someone else; a young occupational therapist, I "put in her place" during one of my hospitalizations for mania; a dietitian, I brought to tears with a frustrated and angry outburst when I found out I had diabetes and the students, I tried to teach my first two years in ministry at St. John's, Elgin, IL. How I longed to love you and share God's love with you and how miserably I often failed. I honestly tried hard, but I was young and inexperienced, and though I did not recognize it at the time, my bipolar condition was raging out of control and you often caught the worst of it. I hope you can forgive me. I love you all and still pray for you!

> *If we claim to be without sin, we deceive ourselves and the truth is not in us. If we confess our sins, he is faithful and just and will forgive us our sins and purify us from all unrighteousness.*
> *(1 John 1:8-9 NIV)*

To God be the Glory for His Amazing Grace in Christ Jesus!

About the Author

"See what great love the Father has lavished on us, that we should be called children of God! And that is what we are!" (1 John 3:1 NIV)

"By this everyone will know that you are my disciples, if you love one another." (John 13:35 NIV)

I am a husband; father; grandfather; uncle; great-uncle; great-great-uncle; son; brother; nephew; cousin; friend; retired Director of Christian Education; ex-theologian; recovering procrastinator, perfectionist and people-pleaser; recovering emotional/binge eater; bipolar disorder and panic attack struggler/survivor/thriver; dreamer/schemer; jack-of-many-trades; seeker and recipient of shalom; sinner/saint; and writer. Encompassing all these things and more, I am a beloved child of God and a follower of Jesus Christ! Sometimes incongruent, controversial, and/or clueless, I am a work in progress! My mission in life is to: "Walk humbly and courageously with God, do good, love and encourage one another!"

I'm passionate about God and people! I strive to follow two main rules in life which I learned many years ago in my work with a children's midweek program:

Rule #1: Treat everyone as a child of God!

Rule #2: See Rule #1.

I also live my life with a deep, dark secret, namely that my name is really, Ralph! Born Ralph Michael Freed, I have always been called, Mike, because my Father and Grandfather were also named Ralph. In fact, it wasn't until I changed schools in 5th grade that I even knew my full name. The teacher was calling the roll and she called, "Ralph?" I didn't answer. "Ralph Freed?" she said, and I sheepishly responded, "That's my dad's name."

I have made peace with the name, Ralph over the years. Ralph means "wolf" or "wolf counsel," Michael means "who is like God" and Freed just means "freed." Put it all together and you get "The Wolf or Wolf-Counsel, who is like God, Freed." I rather like that! It's a great reminder that all of us are freed in Christ to be our best possible selves; the unique and precious beings that God planned for us to be in unity and community with Himself and others! I contemplated listing my full name or the dignified derivative, "R. Michael Freed" as the book's author, but the simplicity and familiarity of "Mike" won out.

My manic vision for this book was of course, that it would become a bestseller! After almost 25 years of false starts and trying to make the book "perfect" it occurred to me (I'm a slow learner at times.) that "done" was perhaps, better than "perfect!" I believe that this revised edition, though still not perfect, is an improvement over the first edition, and as my former therapist often reminded me it's "about progress not perfection!" Though this edition of the book, likely, will not live up to my initial far-fetched expectations either. I remain confident that it, like all of us, is "perfect" for God's purpose and that God will use this book and the author as He sees fit.

I am generally content and happy in my current circumstances and yet, I still occasionally aspire to become a full-time writer and speaker. So, I do my best to discern where God is leading and to follow! And yes, I still hold out hope for a "giraffe cookies and red juice in a ducky cup" continuation of this adventure! (See Chapter 5)

May God bless us and keep us, may He smile upon us and delight in us, may He enable us to grow in love, forgiveness, and understanding of ourselves and others and may He shalom us in His all-encompassing love!

Have I not commanded you? Be strong and courageous. Do not be afraid; do not be discouraged, for the Lord your God will be with you wherever you go." (Joshua 1:9 NIV)

"A new command I give you: Love one another. As I have loved you, so you must love one another." (John 13:34 NIV)

Peace I leave with you; my peace I give you… (John 14:27 NIV)

Created with a Pixabay Image from 947051

(For more by the author, see mikefreed.xyz To contact the author try mikefreed.xyz@gmail.com or call or text his google voice number: 316-285-0473. We will do our best to answer or get back to you.)

Intentional Take-Aways from my Time in Therapy in More-or-Less Random Order

Life is meant to be lived! Sometime life is hard! Be present in the moment! Work for progress not perfection! Keep it simple! Don't be too serious! Beyond a healthy discipline, be gentle with yourself! Small changes when applied consistently over time produce big results! Even with the best preparation, stuff still happens, then we deal with it as best we can with the resources we have at the time! You don't have to wait until Monday to make a change; each day contains multiple opportunities to start fresh, if needed! Sometimes you must accept and live with or through your feelings! That which gets measured gets managed! Swimming (exercise) in moderation is helpful! Be intentional about what you do! You can't be all things for all people! Love, laughter, tears and forgiveness are some of the ingredients of healing! Avoid absolute, catastrophic and negative thinking patterns! Prayer, praise, gratitude and forgiveness are integral to my sense of wellbeing!

I am loved by God! He wants the best for me! He is our refuge and our strength, an ever-present help! Rest, regroup, refocus, but never give up!